Validating Your Business Continuity Plan

Ensuring your BCP really works

Validating Your Business Continuity Plan

Ensuring your BCP really works

ROBERT A. CLARK

IT Governance Publishing

IT Governance Publishing
IT Governance Limited
Unit 3, Clive Court
Bartholomew's Walk
Cambridgeshire Business Park
Ely, Cambridgeshire
CB7 4EA
United Kingdom

www.itgovernance.co.uk

First published in the United Kingdom in 2015
by IT Governance Publishing.

ISBN 978-1-84928-773-9

DEDICATION

This book is dedicated to my brothers John and David.
Both now gone but not forgotten.

ACKNOWLEDGEMENTS

I would like to thank Abdullah Al Hour, AFBCI, Resiliency Consultant at major global IT company, Chris Evans, ITSM specialist and Christopher Wright, Wright-CandA Consulting, for their helpful comments during the review process.

ABOUT THE AUTHOR

In addition to being a Fellow of the Institute of Business Continuity Management, a Member of the Business Continuity Institute and an Approved BCI Instructor, Robert Clark is also a Fellow of the British Computer Society and a Member of the Security Institute. In 1973 he joined IBM as a trainee computer operator. Big Blue was one of those forward thinking organisations that practised business continuity management (BCM) long before the expression had even been coined. But back then, in the 1970s, with the exception of periodic fire evacuation drills, BCM was simply referred to as disaster recovery and was entirely focused on protecting the IT environment, along with the associated electronic data.

It was less than 12 months into his 15 year IBM career that Robert first became exposed to BCM. Both local and overseas disaster fall-back trials were regular features in the IBM calendar and often involved testing recovery capability by transferring UK operations to Germany or the Netherlands. During his time with the corporation, the closest the operation came to a real disaster fall-back was in 1974, during the UK miners' strike, when power interruptions became common place.

Robert's 15 years with IBM were followed by a variety of positions including 11 years with Fujitsu Services (formerly ICL), working with clients on BCM related assignments. In 2005 he was tasked with validating Fujitsu's own BCM state of readiness across Europe. He is now a freelance business continuity consultant and has spent much of the last four years in Malta, where he has promoted BCM both through consultancy assignments and BCI licensed training.

In 2014 Robert became a part-time associate lecturer at Manchester Metropolitan University, where he has been delivering BCM to both undergraduate and postgraduate students, alongside his consultancy commitments. As a member of 'Toastmasters International', he is no stranger to public speaking. An experienced keynote speaker, he often makes use of platforms to promote BCM whenever the opportunities present themselves.

For more information about the author please refer to his website at: *www.bcm-consultancy.com*.

Other publications by the author

Validating Your Business Continuity Plan is Robert Clark's second book. His first, *In Hindsight – A compendium of Business Continuity case studies*, also published by ITGP, went to number one on the Amazon bestseller's lists shortly after its publication in 2014.

He has also had a chapter published in the book: *International Case Studies for Hospitality, Tourism and Event Management Students and Trainees* in 2015 which was entitled: *easyJet Leads the Way on Safer European Air Travel Initiative.*

FOREWORD

If there exists a warm, friendly book about business continuity, then this is it. Reading this book is like having an elderly but very experienced uncle teaching you about the subject, sharing their experience, the lessons they have learned and (business continuity) war stories. It is an easy read, not overly complex, and is sprinkled with anecdotes and lessons learned from Bob's long career in IT and business continuity.

I first met Bob when I was teaching the Business Continuity Institute's (BCI) good practice guidelines in Belfast in 2010. When I think about the course, I am reminded of three events. Firstly, there were only two people on the course, which made the teaching of a four-day course very intense and break-out group work rather difficult! Secondly, the volcanic ash cloud was at its height, so how we all got there I am not too sure. Thirdly, I remember Bob being on the course and I wondered why someone of his experience was on a training course. I think I learned as much from Bob sharing his experiences as he learned from me!

One of the aspects I have enjoyed about *Validating Your Business Continuity Plan* is that it is up to date. This is not some tired old soak in their twilight years writing a book as a vanity project and peddling obsolete business continuity practices. Bob, as shown by coming on the BCI course, keeps himself up to date with the latest business continuity thinking. The book uses all the latest terms, mentions current standards and is just, well, contemporary!

The book is all about validating your business continuity plan, which is part of the business continuity management lifecycle concerned with the practices of exercising, maintaining and reviewing your business continuity programme. As this book states, this is one of the most important parts of business continuity. Without a practiced and tested plan, the rest is worthless. Bob could have just gone for a book on exercising, but I think he makes the subject more complete by talking about the maintenance and review elements as well.

The book covers the need for validating business continuity plans and talks through some of the standards and guidance associated with the subject. It very quickly gets to the meat of the subject by looking at developing exercise programmes. What makes Bob's book slightly different from others is that he comes at exercising from a technical angle as well as from the more standard incident management path that others take. He covers all aspects of exercising and goes into some depth on a number of scenarios, concentrating on media, ICT and terrorism. I thought the information provided in the pandemic case studies was especially interesting and there are a number of other equally insightful case studies. Although the bulk of the book is about exercising, there is a chapter each on maintaining and reviewing a business continuity management system.

Having recently read a couple of other books on business continuity and crisis management, I found Bob's book very different in style. The other recent books were very much textbook-orientated, with lots of 'how to', checklists of considerations, and well-researched, sharp case studies, with every detail double-checked. Bob's is an altogether more approachable style; the case studies' details may not be as sharp but it is easy to dip in and out of the book.

Foreword

It is very much written in the style of teaching the BCI good practice guidelines. It gives the hard facts of how to validate your business continuity plan but also some context in which to place the work and good relevant examples. For those more experienced business continuity professionals, it may not give you any radical new ways of carrying out validation but it will give you reassurance that you are on the right lines and doing the right thing. I would, personally, rather read this type of book on business continuity than others I have tried to read, which were so horribly complex that I didn't get beyond page five. I once met the author of one of the horribly complex business continuity books and immediately asked him to explain what his book was all about. He couldn't make me understand what the book was about either and he looked slightly worried when I suggested he might like to refund me the price of the book!

So, who should read this book? I think it is really aimed at those starting in business continuity and those who have some experience but are looking to gain more. I would also recommend it to those who are taking the good practice guidelines exam and also those who are perhaps carrying out their first few exercises and are looking for reassurance or guidance that they are carrying out best practice. Lastly, I recommend it to anyone who just wants a good read about business continuity – perhaps learn a fact or two, and enjoy the experience of someone who has been doing this since 1974!

Charlie Maclean-Bristol FBCI FEPS
Director
PlanB Consulting
CIR Awards - Business Continuity Consultant of the Year 2011

PREFACE

Validating your business continuity plan (BCP) can be broken down into three component parts – exercising, maintenance and review. In considering each of these three components, this book also takes account of industry standards and guidelines to help steer the reader through the validation process.

"A classic failing of a great many business continuity plans, is that they are written and then left on the shelf." (Drewitt, 2013)

Too many organisations complete their BCPs and then just put them on the shelf to gather dust, without a thought about verifying that the plans actually work. They seem to miss the point that business continuity management is a process of continuous improvement and that the validation phase is a vital constituent part. Moreover, despite the advances that BCM has made in recent years, I still find there are organisations that firmly believe that business continuity is just a computer problem. Consequently, if they do undertake any business continuity planning and validation, it is invariably ICT focused and little else. There is no question that ICT is where business continuity has its roots but organisations that have not recognised that the world has moved on are still living back in the 1970s.

For me, it was in 1974 that I had my first experience, in what was termed a disaster recovery fall-back trial. My IBM colleagues and I had the task of transferring a mission critical IT operation from the UK and proving that it could be successfully recovered and run at an IBM location in Germany. This was intended to assure the continuity of this vital operation should IBM UK's ability to meet its obligations be compromised in any way. The exercise involved hand carrying several boxes of 9-Track 2,400 foot magnetic tapes which even the most advanced only had a capacity of less than 200 megabytes. It is amazing to think that 40 years on the external hard drive that I use for my home computing can comfortably slip into a jacket pocket and has a one terabyte data capacity. The 9-Track tapes contained the vital records that we needed to restore the UK environment for the test at the German host site. These exercises were the only occasions in my life that I can recall ever walking through the red channel at customs, as it was obligatory to declare that we were transporting what was referred to as 'merchandise in baggage'.

I must confess that for someone who has enjoyed a life-long penchant for travel, the prospect of having to spend a long weekend in Germany on expenses was more exciting than the justification for the trip itself. But like so many subsequent business trips I have undertaken, the professional demands took precedence and I never really got the chance to explore the locality. Consequently, I have long since come to regard business travel as an occupational hazard rather than a personal pleasure. One airport departure lounge is much like any other, as have been the hotels that I have stayed in along the way. However, in Germany I did get my first taste of something for which the novelty has never faded and what we now know as business continuity.

If nothing else, my 15 years with IBM emphasised the importance of not only exercising your business continuity plans but ensuring that every employee knew instinctively what part they would have to play in a crisis, even if it was simply 'go home until you are contacted'. Whether the exercise was a simple and inexpensive desk check involving two or three people, or a full blown live rehearsal, it was always taken seriously.

Since that weekend back in 1974, I have literally lost count of the number of BCM exercises and tests that I have been involved with. Some have been straightforward, low cost/low risk exercises, while others have been expensive and risky rehearsals which had the potential of creating a high profile disaster had they gone wrong. And yet, I cannot recall a single test that did not reveal something that needed to be reflected in the business continuity plan under scrutiny. Sometimes all that was necessary was just the dotting of an 'I' or the crossing of a 'T'. In other instances, BCPs have been proved to be inadequate, with substantial rework being needed. It is always better to discover that your plan has flaws during a test, rather than after you have experienced a genuine disaster. It is certainly worth remembering that there are always lessons to be learned and let us not forget that BCM is a process of continuous improvement.

Over the four decades since my initial foray into disaster recovery, I have seen the testing scene maturing in line with the evolution of business continuity. One important point that has long since been apparent to me is that it is virtually impossible to validate every aspect of your plan. To attempt to do so, particularly in a live rehearsal situation, could be creating a disaster of your own making. An exercise programme that defines a controlled and systematic approach, and also one which staggers the activities over a period of time, should be adopted. For some organisations, their exercise programme could extend over several years. Indeed, it is not uncommon for organisations to be regularly rehearsing their BCP, after all, practice does make perfect.

Conversely, you will almost certainly come across those individuals who 'do not have time' to support testing initiatives, or whatever other excuses they choose to present. I have generally found that the inclusion of business continuity as a part of someone's performance objectives, supported by clearly defined and measurable deliverables, will usually do the trick.

In retrospect, I believe it would be true to say that back in the 70s with so much focus on IT disaster recovery, although we did not appreciate it at the time, it was really the tail that was wagging the dog. In fact, some of my IT colleagues even seemed to believe that IT was more important than the business it was intended to support. Such arrogance, or perhaps it was simply naivety? Now, with us well into the 21st century, non-IT based scenarios have long since become a major feature of exercising, as the world has woken up to realise that there is much more to business continuity than just worrying about information technology. Moreover, business continuity has matured into an international standard – ISO22301, although other standards, such as PAS 56 and BS 25999 have played their part along the way in the evolution of the discipline. During that time I have enjoyed working on every phase of the BCM lifecycle and, for some clients, working with them to facilitate the development of their end-to-end business continuity programmes.

Business continuity has no doubt finally come of age with the launching of ISO22301 in 2012 and this book pays due deference to the ISO's criterion. However, in writing the content, it would have been remiss of me to overlook the many years of experience I have gained along the way, coupled with the lessons learned, much of which predates the launching of ISO22301.

CONTENT

Content

Content

LIST OF FIGURES

CHAPTER 1: INTRODUCTION

"One of the oldest axioms within the field of disaster recovery or business continuity planning is that a plan that is not tested or maintained is of little value, or in some cases worse than no plan at all." – (Armit, 2007, p. 323).

The intermittent fire alarm warning sounded. It was not the routine weekly test of the system, scheduled for every Tuesday morning at 10 am. The multi-storey building housed around 500 occupants who instinctively followed standard procedure, cleared their desks, powered off their PCs and prepared to evacuate. Fire wardens donned their high visibility jackets and took up position at their designated stations, including those detailed to assist both pregnant and disabled staff evacuate, should the need arise. Lift vestibules were also manned by wardens to prevent any attempt to use the lifts.

Within two minutes, the fire alarm had changed from an intermittent to a continuous warning signal, thereby heralding an immediate evacuation of the building. Supervised by fire wardens and in an orderly fashion, staff moved promptly to the clearly marked emergency exits. Security personnel manned the exit doors to prevent any unauthorised re-entry, while fire wardens checked that offices, meeting rooms and toilets, etc. were clear.

Staff congregated at their pre-assigned fire assembly points and head count checks were performed, with department managers or their deputies responsible for reporting back to the incident manager. The building reception area staff were responsible for safeguarding the visitor's book during evacuations, to establish each visitor's whereabouts. Any missing members of staff had to be accounted for (e.g. vacation, sick leave, working away from the office, etc.). Had this not been possible, it would be assumed that they were still in the building. As the last report was received, the incident manager checked his stopwatch. Everyone accounted for, including visitors to the building. The evacuation had been completed in nine minutes and 34 seconds – almost one minute inside the target evacuation time. Apart from completing the mandatory post exercise report, along with any recommended actions, the exercise seems to have been successfully concluded – or was it?

Apart from testing how quickly the building could be evacuated, let us also consider what else this exercise may have been trying to achieve. As a bare minimum, an evacuation drill should look to:

- identify any flaws that exist in the evacuation strategy.

- use the opportunity as an awareness exercise for employees who are new, or just unfamiliar with the building selected for the evacuation.

- ensure that the arrangements for any disabled employees or visitors, including any expectant mothers, are properly managed. Remember that the actual number needing assistance may well fluctuate from exercise to exercise.

- monitor the effectiveness of the evacuation from any new building extensions, or from existing areas that may have been subjected to internal structural alterations.

- ensure that any areas with a secure access designation do not in any way compromise the safety of employees, solely in the interest of security[1].
- gauge the effectiveness of communications throughout the building. For example, a public address system announcement may be better heard in some areas than in others.
- consider whether employees' behaviour and attitudes are appropriate. For example:
  - Did everyone take the drill seriously and follow instructions?
  - Did anyone try and use the lifts during the evacuation?
  - Were there any attempts at unauthorised building re-entry?
- solicit both positive and negative feedback from employees, both in terms of the smoothness of the evacuation, as well as the effectiveness of the officials, such as the security personnel and fire wardens. Keep in mind that officials may be negotiating their own learning curve. Also consider whether there were enough officials on duty to carry out the tasks required, especially where evacuating the disabled is concerned.

Whilst a genuine emergency evacuation would give no consideration to the prevailing weather conditions, some leeway can be demonstrated in the case of an exercise. Should the prevailing conditions threaten to be inclement at the time of the proposed exercise, continuing regardless

---

[1] During an evacuation drill, quite by chance, I once found myself trapped in a corridor linking two buildings. The electronic swipe card security system was designed to prevent re-entry after the fire alarm had activated, so I was stopped from entering either building.

may well add an avoidable element of extra risk to the proceedings. Snow and ice, or torrential rain, would not make for ideal conditions and postponing the exercise until conditions are less hazardous may be the most prudent option.

It is perhaps also worth pointing out that this exercise was conducted without any prior warning being given to employees. I have come across business continuity practitioners who argue that you should always provide notice of an intended test. This raises an interesting discussion point, but more about that later in the book.

For other examples of emergency evacuation procedures, anyone who has flown in a commercial aircraft needs only consider the pre-flight safety instruction from the cabin crew. It does not matter whether individuals are experiencing their very first flight, or they have flown hundreds of times, they are still requested to listen and observe while the safety announcements and demonstrations are being carried out. In the event of an emergency, passengers need to know how to behave and how to exit the aircraft as expediently as possible. Cabin crew also need to assess whether the passengers sitting in seats next to emergency exits are, in their opinion, physically capable of opening the exit should the need arise.

As someone who enjoys cruising on a regular basis, I know that one of the first obligatory activities for passengers after embarking is to attend an emergency evacuation drill, which in a live situation could result in the need to abandon ship. Ocean going cruise ships are getting larger and larger, and in some cases the passenger numbers can amount to several thousand. All passengers must report to their pre-allocated muster station, and as part of this rehearsal they need to demonstrate to the safety crew that they can quickly and correctly put on their life jackets before they are dismissed. Practising this 'abandon ship' routine is a massive logistical exercise for the crew. They need to ensure that all passengers are accounted for, and any that fail to appear will be expected to attend a follow up exercise.

Both aircraft and ship's crews will also be directed to engage in regular mandatory training, to ensure that they are capable and competent in dealing with just about any emergency that they are called upon to cope with. In fact, on one recent cruise, I opted to remain on-board while in port and actually observed, first-hand, some of the ship's crew training for a fire scenario – one of the most dangerous threats that ships face.

> *"Around 80 died in the accommodation block from carbon monoxide poisoning while waiting for direction from management."* (Dakin & Jacobsen, 2014, p. 106)

The world is full of tragedies where people have been injured or killed because they did not know what to do when faced with life threatening incidents. Alternatively, they may have found their emergency exit routes blocked, or totally inadequate to deal with the numbers trying to use them. In many instances these tragedies could have been prevented had evacuation procedures been regularly tested, so staff knew what they had to do instinctively.

I personally have been evacuated from two burning offices and from a third office due to the serious risk of an explosion at a neighbouring chemical company's premises. Moreover, I have been evacuated from four hotels in the dead of night when the fire alarm unexpectedly sprang into life. On three occasions it was a false alarm but one was a genuine fire. I don't know about you, but I am never at my best when I am woken up, and it takes a few moments to get my brain into gear. But whenever I check-in to a hotel, I always take the time to find out what and where my emergency evacuation options are before I go to bed. If the lights fail and there is smoke outside your room, knowing which way to go could make the difference between surviving or not.

In 2013, I organised a business continuity and security conference in Malta. One of the case studies was presented by Mario Lentini and concerned an industrial fire that culminated in the creation of an exclusion zone by the Maltese Civil Protection Department (CPD) and which subsequently disrupted those businesses caught within that zone. Lentini was, at the time, responsible for incident management at the Bank of Valletta which had a small self-contained back office business unit based at the site of the fire. The building in question was a multi-occupancy affair which had to be quickly evacuated, especially when smoke started to penetrate their offices through the air conditioning system. Moreover, with the CPD concerned that the smoke was potentially toxic, the evacuation was so rapid that some employees had no opportunity to collect their personal effects resulting in keys, wallets and mobile phones being left in the building. Once outside they were also understandably prevented from recovering their cars from the basement car park beneath the burning building.

During the Q&A session that followed Lentini's presentation, a rather animated debate broke out, as it transpired that a few conference attendees had actually found themselves 'trapped' in an adjacent section of the building from where the fire started. Their designated emergency exit route took them through the premises of other organisations and they discovered their exit route had been obstructed. Fortunately, they found an alternative means of escape. Had an emergency evacuation exercise ever been conducted – apparently not! It also raised the issue of who should actually own a multi-occupancy building evacuation plan, along with the responsibility to periodically exercise the plan.

One final word I would like on this subject is not so much about an evacuation but a lockdown. A situation may transpire that means it may not be safe to actually leave the building you are in. There may, for example, be a shooter on the prowl, or an imminent terrorist threat, in which case you will probably be instructed to lock the doors and keep away from the windows. If there has been a chemical, biological or radiological release in the vicinity, you may be instructed to close all doors and windows and switch off any systems that draw air into the building, while awaiting further instructions.

The only building lockdown I have ever personally experienced was in the UK in 1991 which was necessitated by hurricane force winds. The 14 floor Portsmouth based building was at the time occupied by Zurich Insurance and it literally swayed in the breeze. From my vantage point on the 12th floor, I could see the destruction, particularly to the roofs of other buildings in the area, with the resultant airborne debris making the street a very dangerous place to be. The ground floor reception area had also been hastily turned into a refuge for members of the public caught out in the open, as the conditions had rapidly deteriorated. Fortunately these events are rare in the UK but alas other parts of the world regularly suffer the grief and destruction caused by the adverse weather conditions synonymous with the likes of hurricanes, cyclones and typhoons.

1.1 Unconscious incompetence to unconscious competence

"Business continuity is not so much an add-on or an after-thought, it needs to be a way of life."

So what does all this building evacuation and lockdown stuff have to do with business continuity? Firstly, in my experience, building evacuation rehearsals are probably practiced as much, if not more than, any other situation. Secondly, in the initial building evacuation example on page 21, the organisation in question was rehearsing its emergency evacuation procedure and its effective execution in a genuine situation could literally make the difference between life and death. Probably with the exception of new employees, the staff just reacted to the well-rehearsed exercise in an *'unconscious competence'* state of mind. They did not need to think about what they had to do, they just did it. However, had this evacuation been caused by an incident that left the building unusable (e.g. fire, flood, explosion, toxic chemical release, etc.), thereby creating what is known as a denial of access situation, business continuity plans will be expected to dictate what happens next and how the business will manage the incident.

It is also entirely possible that you could be reacting to instructions from the police. For example, bomb threats are definitely not uncommon, although the ratio of hoaxes to genuine threats seems weighted heavily in favour of the hoax. That said, you cannot afford to ignore these threats and in effect engage in a game equivalent to playing Russian roulette with the health and safety of your employees.

However, the types of incident that can occur are diverse, as are the impacts they can cause an organisation, and many of them are covered later in this book. Moreover, while high profile incidents, such as burning buildings, tend to attract the attention of the media, many of the incidents that organisations may find themselves dealing with will not necessarily be 'headline making' material but could still threaten the survival of unprepared organisations. A business continuity plan will also often be expected to be capable of interfacing with other plans, such as emergency evacuation plans or pandemic plans. If an organisation has already created these plans when it develops its BCP, there is no point in re-inventing the wheel and duplicating what already exists. But the organisation needs to ensure that these plans are joined up and will work alongside each other. This is where validation can certainly help.

The 2010 edition of the Business Continuity Institute's Good Practice Guideline (BCI, 2010, p. 41) identifies four levels of staff awareness which can be defined as:

1. *'Unconscious Incompetence'* where staff are unaware of BCM issues and they do not know what they do not know.
2. *'Conscious Incompetence'* where staff are aware of BCM generally, but know little about its detailed requirements.
3. *'Conscious Competence'* where staff are cognisant of the BCM issue and are proficient (e.g. in following documented procedures) in supporting BCM.
4. *'Unconscious Competence'* where staff are instinctively fully competent in applying BCM in a variety of circumstances.

Most organisations will first engage with business continuity when their staff are at the lowest level of awareness – *'Unconscious Incompetence'*. Their objective should be to attain the highest level through a variety of methods, such as exercising their BCP, training, awareness campaigns and rehearsals. Exercising fosters teamwork and collaboration between diverse areas of an organisation, while developing proficiency, confidence and knowledge as it levitates the overall level of competence. Moreover, the organisation's confidence in its own ability to manage incidents will profit too.

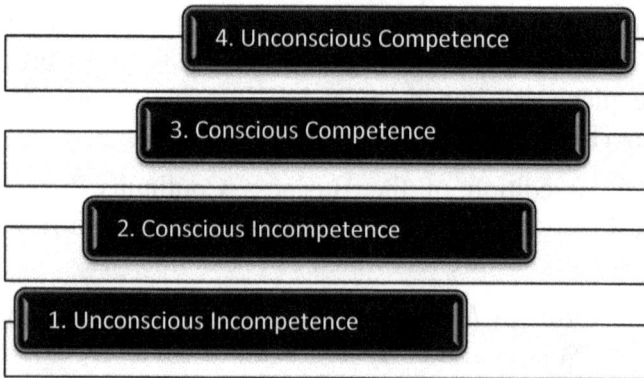

Figure 1: The four BCM 'levels of competence'

In fact, testing, validation, exercising or rehearsals are all variations of a common theme and, in addition to proving that a business continuity plan works as intended, they would certainly be expected to play an important part of its development towards that desired level of *'Unconscious Competence'*.

> *"An untested plan is only a strategy."* Richard Gagnon, 2007

Organisations that choose not to validate their BCP will not only miss the opportunity to improve the organisation's level of BCM competence, but arguably, the BCP itself will be worthless. It does not matter how much it cost you to develop, or how much attention to detail you pay in preparing your BCP, if it is not validated, it will simply not be worth the paper it is printed on.

1.2 The benefits of effective validation

For some organisations, the investment required in developing its business continuity response will have been substantial. Once a BCP has been produced, unless a good understanding and appreciation exists amongst its sponsors for the need for validation, along with a commitment to continuous improvement, a BCM programme can stall.

> *"A continuity plan without realistic testing is not only useless – it is also a complete waste of money."*
> Herve Riou

From a validation perspective, it is perhaps a good moment to remind ourselves of its importance. But before focusing specifically on validation, I would like to share something that I was reminded of recently. It relates to a survey conducted by the Chartered Management Institute amongst its membership. Entitled 'Planning for the worst', it quizzed members on their business continuity management. Two of the findings particularly stood out for me:

> *"The most compelling finding in this year's survey is that 81% of managers whose organisations activated their business continuity arrangements in the last 12 months say that it was effective in reducing disruption.*
>
> *The same number agree that the cost of developing BCM is justified by the benefits it brings their organisation."* (Pearson & Woodman, 2012, p. 14)

With such a large percentage of the participants believing that the benefits derived justify the cost, one significant interpretation from the second paragraph is that, if properly applied, BCM can be cost neutral.

Whether your organisation is a large multinational corporation or a SME, validation is still a critical component of the BCM process. So what exactly are we trying to achieve by applying validation? From a high-level perspective, we should be looking to demonstrate that all information in the plan(s) has been confirmed, the plan(s) has been fully rehearsed, and all appropriate employees and their nominated deputies have also been involved in the exercises. With every exercise undertaken, the workforce should be moving closer to that goal of reaching 'Unconscious Competence', while instilling a greater level of confidence in both management and workforce alike. It will also serve to raise the level of awareness across the organisation.

Validation will be broken down into more detail later in the book, as it takes the reader through a logical approach to exercising business continuity plans from a simple desk check, through to a live rehearsal. It will consider the standards and guidelines that are available, while providing examples of actual testing – some of which worked well and some of which did not. Case studies have also been included that look at how organisations have dealt with exercising their BCPs to address a variety of threats, such as:

- Civil unrest
- Cyber attacks
- Denial of access
- Discovery of white powder in a mail delivery
- Exclusion zones

- Explosion
- IT/telco failure
- Loss of staff/expertise
- Pandemics
- Power failure
- Terrorism (including 9/11 type scenario, bomb threats, WMD threat, plus a college campus gunman threat).

Examples are also given in section 5.1, where reputational damage was caused by atrocious media communication in three actual live situations. However, before getting into the 'nuts and bolts' of BCP validation, the book will consider the argument that business continuity should actually start at home in *Chapter 3*. Many of us, even those individuals who perhaps do not consider themselves to be well versed in its methods, conceivably already practice BCM without actually realising it.

1.3 Why do we need to exercise our BCP?

"Validation is the Professional Practice within the BCM Lifecycle that confirms that the BCM Programme meets the objectives set in the BC Policy and that the organisation's BCP is fit for purpose." (BCI, 2013, p. 94).

Once a BCP has been developed, it still remains theoretical until such times as it can be proved that it works, by subjecting it to an effective validation programme. Unfortunately, this will be considered by some ill-informed executives as an unnecessary overhead that is rarely of the highest priority, and it will invariably take its place behind whatever happens to be considered as the issue of the day. I am constantly amazed by executives who dismiss the inherent dangers associated with not validating their BCPs as being irrelevant. Back in the late 1990s, I witnessed this happen with monotonous regularity with the various Year 2000 programmes I worked on. With the benefit of hindsight, we can argue that the Y2K threat was grossly overrated hype. Even so, we did not necessarily know that at the time, and with the immoveable deadline getting ever closer, I found some executives still reluctant to engage with the process. To save time, one executive I had the dubious pleasure of working for, even wanted the team to modify suspect computer software and reinstall it into the live environment without testing it first. This was not a shrewd plan and had we concurred he would have undoubtedly been the first to complain should we have ended up creating more problems than we fixed.

But to not validate your BCP, not only serves to devalue its currency, but it also creates the very serious and avoidable risk that it will not perform if and when called upon to do so. This begs the question – *'Is your BCP really worth the paper it's printed on?'* If you have not validated the plan, there can only be one answer – 'No'.

So apart from recognising that business continuity management is a holistic process, and that validation is an integral part of that process, let us consider some of the benefits derived from exercising your BCP:

- Ensuring that the BCP is fit for purpose, while providing the opportunity to make any amendments or additions to reflect those aspects of the BCP that did not perform as well as expected.

- Authentication of the strategies used to develop the BCP, while verifying that existing business priorities have been acknowledged.

- Confirmation that recovery time objectives can be met, especially in the face of a multiple scenario incident.

- Training employees, including their deputies, in the execution of their respective business continuity roles and responsibilities, by designing realistic scenarios and integrating role playing as part of the exercise.

- Raising the level of awareness of business continuity within the organisation.

- Increasing stakeholder confidence in the organisation's ability to respond to an incident.

- Achieving buy-in and plan ownership from the business areas.

- Assessing whether any organisational changes, including those resulting from acquisitions or mergers, can be accommodated within the constraints of the current business continuity arrangements.

- Testing of those components that require a 'pass' or 'fail' result, such as generators.

- Ensuring that ICT disaster recovery plans can meet recovery time objectives, especially for multiple system failures.

Before your business continuity plans can be signed off as fully operational, along with any associated plans, such as ICT disaster recovery plan, pandemic plan, emergency evacuation plan, etc., it must be demonstrated as being fit for purpose via a structured validation programme.

1.4 Does everyone need to validate their BCP?

The Business Continuity Institute's 2013 Good Practice Guidelines identifies six acceptable strategies that can be adopted as part of your business continuity arrangements:

1. **Diversification:** necessitates identical activities being performed at two or more physically remote locations, such that if work at one location is interrupted, it continues at the other(s).

2. **Replication**: is similar to diversification except that the replicated site is dormant and only becomes operational after an incident. It will generally need staff to be relocated to the replica following an incident.

3. **Standby**: assumes the availability of a facility that can be made ready to recommence business activities within the recovery time objective (RTO) which is assumed to be greater than a day.

4. **Subcontracting**: by using a third party supplier to take over the provision of a service or the manufacture of a product that your organisation offers, or the provision of ICT services, such as disaster recovery facilities.

5. **Post incident acquisition**: assumes the procuring of resources needed to take on activities after an incident. This would usually be driven by pre-prepared lists of requirements and should only be selected as a strategy for RTOs measured in days or weeks.

6. **Do nothing**: implies the luxury of time to decide how to deal with the effects that an incident has caused after the event.

The first three strategies listed and possibly 'subcontracting' too, would generally be adopted by organisations with short RTOs that are measured in days or even hours. Number '5' – 'post incident acquisition', would be considered an acceptable strategy for organisations with RTOs measured in weeks. Finally, the 'do nothing' strategy is what you might expect organisations to select when they really have the luxury of time on their side and RTOs that are measured in months. I have, in fact, from time to time come across a seventh strategy which is a dependency upon what is probably most appropriately referred to as 'divine intervention'. However, in my humble opinion this is analogous to strategy number 6 – i.e. 'Do nothing'.

The BCI good practice guidelines (GPG) also point out that the sixth strategy is the default option for those organisations that are yet to implement business continuity. It implies that organisations electing to opt for this default are assuming that they will have months to respond to an incident. The truth may be that they really do not know how much time they have, particularly if they have not completed a business impact analysis. Given these circumstances, this makes option '6' a potentially dangerous option, especially if you do not know how much time you have to recover your organisation before it could find its very survival placed in serious jeopardy.

So let us consider the question of 'Do we really need to validate our BCP?'. To my mind, if any of the first four strategy options are used as input to your BCP development, the answer is a no-brainer – 'Yes', you must validate your plan. As for the post incident acquisition, while it may not be possible to perform any live exercises due to the very nature of the strategy, all other types of exercise (see Section 4.2.1) should be considered. Finally, I have to admit that undertaking any kind of exercise would be very difficult for the 'Do nothing' strategy, particularly if you intend to wait until after an incident to decide what to do. How can you define an exercise based upon key decisions that you are yet to make?

"As a simple rule, if it has not been tested it does not work." (Armit, 2007, p. 324)

I hope you have already got the message that a business continuity plan that has not been validated should be considered as nothing more than a strategy. So you can only really say you have a BCP in place once it has been validated. Moreover, the BCI provide us with some rather alarming company failure statistics:

• **25% of companies never reopen following a disaster**
• **80% of companies that have not recovered within one month are likely to go out of business**
• **75% of companies without a business continuity plan in place are likely to fail within three years**

Figure 2: Percentage of companies that go out of business
Source (The BCI Video – The Time is Now)

Effectively validating your BCP can only enhance the likelihood of successfully dealing with an incident and improve your organisation's chances of not becoming just a 'statistic'. Like fire drills, practice makes perfect, and ensures the ongoing development of employee awareness and organisational readiness. This is complemented by the flexibility to try out multiple scenarios, providing ample opportunities for dress-rehearsals – particularly if they are performed unannounced. Any flaws in the BCP will be detected, and rest assured that validation affords us a far less risky approach than waiting to exercise the plans with a real incident!

As a consultant, I have occasionally been asked which industries business continuity applies to. The answer of course is that it is not industry specific. I have personally worked in a variety of industries, plus the public sector. Some exercises would be very similar, such as validating cyber defences, or dealing with a pandemic, regardless of the industry. However, other exercises undertaken will vary from industry to industry, simply because of the very nature of the businesses they operate. For example, retail banks will want to ensure that they can still offer deposit and withdrawal services to customers when there has been an ICT failure. Conversely, a manufacturer may want to validate contingencies that they may have in place that perhaps outsource the manufacture of key products while waiting for damaged plant equipment replacements. The ICT failure may be something that can be resolved relatively quickly, whereas the lead time for replacement plant equipment could take months, as it may need to be built to order, rather than being an off the shelf item. What all these organisations from different industries have in common is the need to validate and maintain their business continuity plans. Despite the inherent differences of their respective end products and services, the validation methods and approach they each use should be comparable.

Since the evolution of business continuity management from its ICT disaster recovery roots, organisations have come to realise that, while their ICT infrastructure remains a vital part of the overall jigsaw, it is only part of what they need to protect. In fact, the entire organisation needs to reach the position where business continuity becomes just a way of life, regardless of their size or raison d'être.

1.5 In the beginning there was a flood

"The Founder of Recovery Planning was Noah, but he had good connections and prior warning ... we do not!" Melvyn Musson (Continuity Central, 2006)

Over the past few years, I have seen some fairly frequent references to Noah and his alleged contribution towards business continuity. Moreover, I have also noted that it has been suggested that Noah should be considered a role model by your average business continuity professional. After all, there are those who would argue that building the Ark and saving the world's animal population from drowning, was indeed the first recorded instance of business continuity in action. It certainly predates the evolution of IT disaster recovery which is the generally accepted origin of what we now acknowledge as modern business continuity. That said, there are accounts that lead us to believe that Noah finished the Ark's construction just before the rains fell, suggesting that perhaps he was working to a plan driven by some sort of sacred deadline.

But let's just take a step back for a moment. Is this role model status really justified when all said and done, until recently, I for one had never actually seen any evidence that he ever exercised his plan? With the rain falling and the flood waters rising, it would not have been a good time to have discovered that the plan had been dangerously flawed in some way. History has since provided examples of ships that were discovered not to be fit for purpose when they capsized and sank. Two cases that come to mind are King Henry VIII's flagship *Mary Rose* that was lost in 1545 and the Swedish ship the *Vasa* which capsized in 1628. In the latter case, the ship sank on its maiden voyage. Let us also not forget the 1912 Titanic catastrophe. Despite being considered by many to be unsinkable, the ship was clearly never stress tested for iceberg collisions.

We could of course debate whether the story of Noah and the Ark is actually fact or fiction. However, assuming for a moment that there is some truth in the account, I guess in his defence I should relate to one explanation that I came across while researching for this book. It suggested that when the Ark was constructed, Noah actually had no knowledge of the impending flood.

> *"The Ark was not built as a lifeboat. It was built long before the flood as a commercial river barge for transporting cattle, grain, and other cargo."* (Best, 1999)

Best claims that the Ark had been sailed up and down the River Euphrates, in what is now modern day Iraq, long before the flooding occurred. This being the case, I stand corrected, as Noah did, at the very least, test that the Ark would float and with a host of animals on board too! Of course, this account does challenge the story of Noah building the Ark, by suggesting that it was never built in response to a divine command.

CHAPTER 2: STANDARDS AND GUIDELINES

"Validation is the process of assuring your readiness for a disruptive event or crisis." – (Sterling, et al., 2012, p. 171)

By adopting a set of standards or guidelines and applying them to business continuity, organisations ensure that they approach BCM in a consistent manner. This naturally applies to validation, as much as any other aspects of BCM. There are an abundance of options available to select from, including the international standard ISO22301. However, in the case of this standard, it is not the intent to define a rigid structure on which a business continuity management system (BCMS) must be based. Indeed, it provides a flexible framework enabling organisations to create a BCMS which is suitable for their requirements. In recognising that one size does not fit all, organisational needs are influenced by several factors including legal and organisational niceties. Some organisations will also be regulated and have to follow a predetermined standard or set of guidelines. This chapter takes a look at some of the options including giving due consideration to the more modest BCM needs of the small and medium size enterprises (SMEs).

2.1 What is in a name?

"What's in a name? That which we call a rose by any other name would smell as sweet." Romeo and Juliet (II, ii, 1-2)

Any research for the definition of 'validation' in a business continuity context will invariably yield a variety of explanations which may appear to be a variation around a common theme. A number of frequently occurring verbs will be encountered – exercise, test, rehearse, train, etc. But what exactly are we trying to do – are we testing, rehearsing or exercising our BCPs? What exactly is in a name and are they really different or are they interchangeable? Is it a case of one is right and another is wrong? I have to be honest and say that through the force of a habit developed over several decades, I tend to use the word 'testing' more often than 'exercising'. From a BCM viewpoint is this 'politically correct'? I have to admit the answer is 'No', it is not.

There are a variety of answers to be found in the copious standards, good practice guidelines, or books that are available. But in considering the answer to these questions, I decided to reference the words in a thesaurus. A number of common words were presented (e.g. trial, try-out, run-through, assessment, preparation, training, etc.). However, what quickly became apparent was that a single common denominator is the word *'practice'* which immediately reminded me of the old adage that *'practice makes perfect'*. Not a bad start when you consider organisations should be aiming to achieve a level of 'unconscious competence' in the execution of their BCPs. Without practising they will simply never achieve this.

> *"Exercises can be used for validating policies, plans, procedures, training, equipment, and inter-organisational agreements; testing information and communication technology (ICT) disaster recovery systems; clarifying and training personnel in roles and responsibilities; improving inter-organisational*

co-ordination and communications; identifying gaps in resources; improving individual performance; identifying opportunities for improvement; and, providing a controlled opportunity to practice improvisation. " (ISO22398, 2012, p. 7)

This extract from ISO22398 suggests that exercising in a BCM context is multi-faceted and testing is actually a component part of an exercise programme. Testing is typically an exercise from which you expect a 'pass' or 'fail' outcome. For example, did the generator kick-in when the power supply was interrupted, or was the building successfully evacuated within the target timeframe? A 'pass' will earn you a tick in the box, while a 'fail' should lead to the inevitable question – 'why did it fail?'. Conversely, for an exercise that is also being used as a training opportunity, you would probably want to avoid a 'pass' or 'fail' situation, or any attempt to attribute blame. In the aftermath of an exercise, taking account of what went well and what needs improving as part of a learning exercise, would be much more appropriate.

In my early days of IT disaster recovery experience at IBM, we would transfer the operation to Germany or the Netherlands, and perform a parallel run of something that had already been completed in the UK in a business as usual mode. In this way, we always knew precisely what results to expect. While there were always other lessons to be learned, the key test was did the disaster recovery test produce the same results as the original UK run? Had the answer been 'No', then questions would have been asked.

So, in summary, we must remember that different objectives dictate different terms. A <u>Test</u> is a pass/fail activity. An <u>Exercise</u> is an activity objected for enhancement. A

Rehearsal is an activity for building familiarity while Training is an activity for building specific skills. Some BCM professionals may argue that it doesn't matter what you call it – the important thing is to make sure that you validate your BCP! However, in this instance, careful definition terminology within your organisation will reduce the risk of embarrassing misunderstandings, or even worse.

2.2 Regulations, legislations, standards and good practice

In January 2015, the Business Continuity Institute published a very interesting report on International BCM Legislations, Regulations, Standards and Good Practice Guidelines. *"This document was created in response to requests received by the BCI from its members and other interested parties about current legislation, regulation and standards that exist nationally and internationally for Business Continuity Management."* (Byrd, 2015).

The report presents both an international view, plus a consolidated picture from the 40 or so countries represented. What immediately struck me is the disparity between countries in terms of the number of these governance documents that each utilises across the four categories (e.g. legislations, regulations, standards and good practice, etc.). The US leads the way with 42 documents but many of the countries included in the report have only a single document in place which in most instances is regulation targeting banks and the financial sector.

Type of Governance	International	US	UK	Australia	Canada	Netherlands	China	Italy
Legislations	2	18	1	1	2	0	0	1
Regulations	3	19	1	9	2	2	3	1
Standards	29	14	15	6	2	1	1	0
Good practices	8	25	6	10	2	1	1	0
TOTAL	42	76	23	26	8	4	5	2

Figure 3: Legislation, regulation, standards and good practice comparisons

The report also provides a demonstration of the inconsistencies between nations of how extensively BCM is applied across the different sectors.

• Banking and finance	• Industry – general
• Public health and healthcare	• Agriculture, food supply and water
• Transportation and shipping	• Information distribution and communications
• Energy (including nuclear)	• Government and public agencies

Figure 4: Sectors covered by BCM governance

2.3 The ISO22301 BCMS family of standards

Unlike my early days at IBM, there are now globally accepted standards and guidelines to help with the negotiation of the trials and tribulations associated with not only validating a BCP but with all matters relating to business continuity management. In fact, when I first got involved with BCM in 1974, we still had almost 30 years to wait for the first publically available standard – PAS 56, which was launched in 2003.

With so many businesses detrimentally affected, culminating in around 600,000 job losses, the 9/11 terrorist attacks in 2001 were a major factor in emphasising the importance of BCM globally. This was further accentuated by the subsequent launching of BS 25999 in 2006, which was adopted as the established BCM standard across many parts of the globe. Finally, after evolving for around 40 years, 2012 saw BCM come of age, when it joined the ranks of the international standards, taking its place alongside the likes of quality management and risk management. The new business continuity management system, or ISO22301 as it is known, was up and running.

The ISO22301 family now includes a number of BCM standards which includes:

Designation	Description
BS ISO22300: 2012	Societal security: Terminology
BS ISO22301: 2012	Societal security: Business continuity management systems – Requirements
BS ISO22313: 2012	Societal security: Business continuity management systems – Guidance
BS ISO22398: 2013	Societal security: Guidelines for exercises

Figure 5: List of relevant BCMS ISO family of standards

While this family of standards continues to evolve, arguably the most relevant family member for 'validating your BCP', is ISO22398. However, it is not the intent to reproduce that publication throughout these pages, but readers of this book may also find this standard useful additional reading.

Not every organisation needs to go down the ISO22301 route, as adhering to its dictates may create a business continuity management system which is far more complex than an organisation needs or could justify. However, that said, achieving ISO22301 certification may possibly be a prerequisite criterion that one of your clients insists on you accomplishing if you wish to do business with them. I am aware of a number of small and medium sized enterprises (SMEs) that have had BS 25999, and more recently ISO22301, effectively imposed upon them in this way.

However, those organisations that are seeking to achieve or retain their ISO22301 status, will need to demonstrate to the certification body that their BCMS has been correctly implemented and is compliant with the standard. Moreover, they must demonstrate that they are meeting the validation criterion that the ISO defines. To achieve these high standards compromise is not an option.

2.4 The Business Continuity Institute's good practice guidelines

The report mentioned in section 2.2 refers to the various legislations, regulations, standards and good practices that are applied to BCM across the globe. With regard to the latter, although there are several different guidelines listed, for three reasons I have elected to talk specifically about the BCI's good practice guidelines (GPG).

1. The BCI's GPG is recognised internationally, and it is also listed by many countries as the guidelines of choice.

It has now been translated from the original English into Arabic, French, German, Italian, Korean, Spanish and US English, with Chinese and Japanese versions also in the pipeline.

2. The BCI's GPG are the guidelines that I am most familiar with and regularly reference in my consultancy work.

3. Finally, as an Approved BCI Instructor, the licensed courses I have delivered for the BCI's certificate (CBCI) have been based on the BCI's GPG.

Figure 6: The business continuity management lifecycle
Source: (BCI, 2013, p. 13)

The Business Continuity Institute published its first version of its good practice guidelines in 2002, with the 2013 GPG version being closely aligned to ISO22301.

These guidelines have also become the basis for preparing candidates to sit the BCI's certificate examination from which successful candidates are awarded the post nominal and industry recognised CBCI – Certificate of the Business Continuity Institute, a 'Level 4' qualification.

Described within the GPG is the business continuity management lifecycle which defines two management practices (*policy and programme management* plus *embedding*), supported by four technical practices (*analysis, design, implementation* and *validation*). This book focuses on the validation practice which enables an organisation to establish that its BCP's objectives are met, while determining that the plan is fit for purpose.

In Section 2.1 – 'What's in a name?', I acknowledged that the force of a longstanding habit has resulted in me using the word 'test', when 'exercise' would often have been more appropriate. The same can also be applied to the terminology used within the GPG and the way it has evolved over the last ten years. One could be forgiven for making the same kind of mistake that I am prone to make regarding 'test' and 'exercise'.

In the following table, you will note not only the different terms used for the various aspects of exercising, but also that none of the terms used in 2005 survived beyond the 2010 edition of the GPG.

Exercise terminology used	BCI good practice guidelines edition			
	2005	2008	2010	2013
Desk check	Y	Y	Y	
Discussion based				Y
Walkthrough	Y	Y	Y	
Table top				Y
Simulation exercises	Y	Y	Y	
Unit test			Y	
Unit rehearsal			Y	
End-to-end test			Y	
Functions	Y			
Activity testing		Y		
Command post				Y
Full test	Y	Y	Y	
Live				Y

Figure 7: Evolution of GPG exercise terminology

Interestingly enough, ISO22398 further breaks down the term 'discussion based' into a further four sub categories:

- Seminar
- Workshop
- Table top exercise
- Discussion based game.

2.5 Small and medium size enterprise considerations

Despite the existence of ISO22301 and the BCI's good practice guidelines, not to mention the plethora of other means of governance available globally, some small and medium size enterprises (SMEs) may argue that applying either could be considered an overkill, even though organisations of all sizes should embrace BCM, if only in the interest of self-preservation. With SMEs in mind, and endorsed by the UK Cabinet Office and the BCI, the book *'Business Continuity for Dummies'* was published. I believe that it is best described as a 'light' version of the BCI's GPG. Even so, the title should in no way be taken as an affront on the readers' intellectual capabilities, as it is simply designed to appeal to those SMEs that considered a full-blown business continuity management system to be unnecessary.

Chapter 11 addresses validation and it makes the distinction between 'exercising' and 'testing' as the former being multifaceted, while the latter would typically give a 'pass' or 'fail' result. However, what is noticeably missing are references to auditing your BCMS, which is an integral part of the BCI GPG and a compulsory aspect of achieving ISO22301 certification.

2.6 Quality assurance

Several years ago, a gentleman by the name of Charles Rutt was a director at Barclays Bank, and he was also the sponsor of a programme I was managing for the bank. During my time there, he once referred to me as a 'quality zealot'. It was meant as a compliment and it was taken in the same spirit. So perhaps you will understand why I make no apologies for labouring the point about quality in this section.

The first universally recognised standard I ever came across in my career was the British Standard for Quality Management (QM) which was given the designation BS 5750. This was during my time at IBM, and the experience

I gained has held me in good stead ever since, regardless of the various roles I have performed over the years. I believe it is true to say that the implied quality philosophy practiced at IBM was in line with the words of W. Edward Deming – *"Quality is everyone's responsibility"*.

It was about the time that BS 5750 was morphing into the ISO9000 family of standards that I was invited to meet a prospective client who was interested in commissioning some consultancy work. I understood he wanted to meet me to check my suitability for the work he had in mind, before signing any agreements with my organisation. So in a sense, this was a kind of job interview – something that happens from time to time in the consultancy world. He asked me to express my view of the statement that *'quality management was an overhead'*. My response was along the lines of *"No, I don't believe it to be an overhead, I consider it to be an investment"*. That was apparently the answer that he was looking for, and shortly after we met he signed the agreement. I must admit that, at the time, I thought the question was a little out of left field, as the consultancy work he was after was business continuity related rather than quality management. However, after having begun the consultancy assignment, I subsequently learned that taking me on had hinged on the answer I gave. Apparently, the consultants he had met from the three or four organisations he had shortlisted, had provided a variety of answers, none of which had impressed him.

Nevertheless, much as I believe in the importance of quality management, I always find it something of an enigma that just because an organisation has an ISO9000 certification, it does not guarantee that its products or services are of a good quality, although I have no doubt that it helps. But how can that be? Perhaps I am being too cynical, but by adhering to the international standard, what organisations are doing is demonstrating that they follow a consistent set of processes in creating their products or delivering their services. They, in turn, may be of a good, bad, or indifferent quality, but at least the method of their creation or delivery is always uniform.

Towards the end of my time with IBM, the corporation launched the A/S 400 mid range computer that revolutionised the world of information technology. To say that the quality control applied to the operating system software was rigorous, is something of an understatement. It is generally accepted that the earlier a fault is detected in the software development lifecycle, the easier and cheaper it is to fix. This observation is not solely restricted to the world of software development, and it certainly gives credence to the old saying that '*a stitch in time saves nine*'.

Back in the late 1980s, the cost of that A/S 400 quality assurance programme was in the region of $250,000. However, the faults that were discovered in the software and corrected in its pre-release state, saved IBM an estimated figure that was in excess of $5,000,000 – the approximate cost of having to correct those faults once the A/S 400s had been shipped to customers. From a cost avoidance perspective, this meant that for every dollar IBM spent on the quality assurance programme, the corporation's saving was $20. Not a bad return on investment.

So does quality management have a part to play in business continuity? Even though the words '*quality*' or '*ISO9000*' barely get a mention in ISO22301, in my view the answer is a 'no-brainer' – 'Yes', of course it does. In contrast, the

Business Continuity Institute's Good Practice Guidelines make frequent reference to quality management and quality assurance throughout the BCM lifecycle. I look upon the BCP validation process as a vital part of that quality assurance, as it helps ensure your BCP is, and remains, fit for purpose. However, there is one particular lesson I learned with BS 5750 that still holds true, and which most definitely applies to your business continuity – *"You cannot test quality into your product or service, you can only demonstrate that it is or is not there"*.

Put another way, if you make mistakes or omissions in the BCM analysis, design and/or the implementation phases of your business continuity programme, validation will only flag them, it will not correct them. What validation will do for you is to identify those aspects of your BCP where quality is poor, or is absent all together, and which may well require some rework somewhere in the upstream BCM lifecycle. It is all part of the continuous improvement process. It is far better to find out that your BCP has flaws during some form of validation, than make this discovery when an incident occurs.

Support for this argument can be found from within the business continuity ISO family, as ISO22398 advises us that:

> *"Exercises are an important management tool intended to identify gaps and areas for improvement as well as to determine the effectiveness of response and recovery strategies. In addition to measuring the competence of the organisation and its personnel, exercises are excellent tools to assess revised plans and changed programmes for completeness, relevancy and accuracy."* (ISO22398, 2012, p. 7)

I have come across a number of organisations during my career that have believed that if they include a token testing phase (or in the case of BCM, validating the plan) at the end of any development project, then they can forego the need for any upstream quality assurance. Wrong! While the testing or validation phase is vital, the earlier you can detect a fault, the quicker and less costly it will be to resolve. Business continuity is no different. Consider the lesson that the IBM A/S 400 operating system quality assurance programme provides, as mentioned earlier in this section.

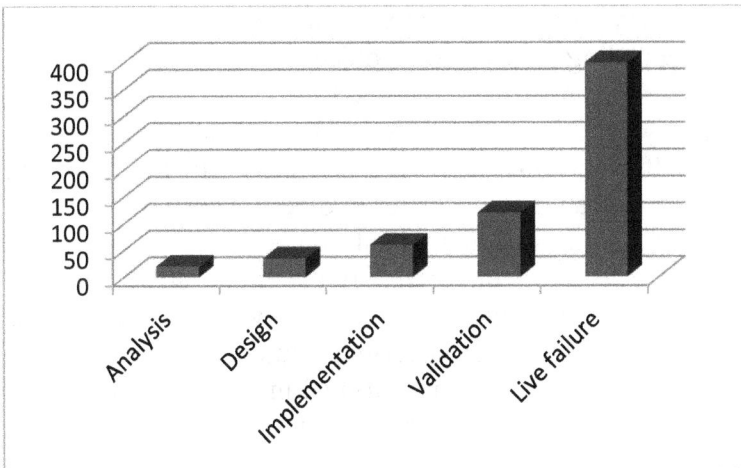

Figure 8: Comparative costs of correcting errors in BCM lifecycle

For example, I believe that most, if not all, business continuity professionals will agree that the business impact analysis is the foundation stone on which the BCMS is built. Get this wrong and everything else that follows will be wrong too. Likewise, if a strategy is created and it is then used to develop a BCP, if the strategy is defective in some way, or it is based upon some unproven assumptions, those defects will be reflected in the BCP. So what I am advocating is that quality assurance needs to be applied to each of the practices within BCM and not just included as part of the validation process.

Now the good news is that you may have already been applying quality assurance techniques in your BCMS, as sometimes it is all about employing straightforward common sense. If you consider the deliverables from the business impact analysis (BIA), has a maximum tolerable period of disruption (MTPD) been recorded and signed-off for every urgent activity? Do they each have a corresponding recovery time objective (RTO)? However, if, for example, you have recorded the value of a MTPD as two days and it should have been two weeks, the strategy and ultimate BCP response is likely to be far more expensive than it needs to be. In other words, you will have created a solution which is substantially and unnecessarily over-engineered. Conversely, if the figure should be two days and it has been recorded as two weeks, the reverse is true, and the resulting under-engineered solution could, in fact, put the organisation's survival in serious jeopardy if it was ever subjected to a live incident.

I have seen this happen in reality very recently, when an ICT solution had been designed and implemented around the parameters defined, as it was later discovered, incorrectly during the BIA. This organisation's computing department subsequently effectively demonstrated that it could complete a disaster recovery fall-back to its recovery site within two hours of an interruption. All very impressive, except that a two day recovery timeframe would have been more than adequate for what the business really needed.

Certainly two of the relatively uncomplicated QA activities which will be ongoing throughout the BCM lifecycle are:

1. Does all the documentation meet the organisation's documentation control standards (please refer to Section 8.4 – Managing your documentation)?
2. Ensure that all the relevant boxes have been ticked. For example, has the management team agreed and signed off the various strategies being proposed by the resultant BCPs? As the name suggests, the BCP is a plan, so a QA check would be appropriate to verify that all necessary resources have been identified and allocated. Some may argue that this is basic project management stuff but the important point is that it gets done.

From a QA perspective, I would always recommend walking through the strategies once they have been designed. This may not be a train of thought that all my fellow business continuity professionals would necessarily endorse but I believe that it is better to find that your strategies have a flaw, however big or small, before you commence with the development of your BCP(s) rather than afterwards.

Finally, quality assurance will verify that the deliverables from the BCM programme will conform to the organisation's requirements which ideally should have been formally pre-defined, documented and signed off. Moreover, organisations that are, or intend to become, certified against an international or national standard, QA will ensure that the prerequisite criterions are met and adhered to.

CHAPTER 3: BUSINESS CONTINUITY BEGINS AT HOME

"The disaster that impacts your company may also impact employee's homes – make sure continuity plans include alternate workforce options." – Joe Flach

I was recently reading a newspaper report about 30,000 people in Scotland who were into their third day without any electricity. Overhead power lines had been brought down by heavy weather that had pounded the north of the United Kingdom. Now as I write, snow is falling outside my window, media broadcasts warn of roads in the locality being gridlocked and nearby Manchester airport has been closed while snowploughs sweep the runway. All this reminded me of an instance back in the 1980s when I lived in a small village in a rural area in the south of England and I also went for more than three days without power. On that occasion, snow and ice was the culprit and having no electricity in the middle of winter is no joke, particularly as the temperature did not rise above freezing during the power outage.

No electric lighting in the house or streets, no power to run central heating pumps or boil a kettle, and if you used electricity to cook with, you were really in trouble. Moreover, while some local shops struggled on as best they could, filling up the car with fuel was problematical, as the petrol stations in the vicinity were also without power. A local hotel was reported to be struggling to keep open as, even though it was appropriately stocked with candles and had an abundant supply of bottled liquid petroleum gas (LPG) for cooking and heating, it needed electricity to pump water from a well. It was during this period that I also attended a local wedding. I have to say that the church was beautifully decorated with flowers and candles, and I am sure that the gas heaters which had been drafted in had made it feel warmer than if the power had been on. Of course the organ was not working either which made the quality of the singing rather 'interesting'.

All that said, during those three days, my family and I were quite warm and comfortable in the house, enjoying regular hot meals, even though we normally used electricity for cooking. We had an abundant supply of candles, torches and gas lanterns, the latter two which we generally used for our summer camping forays. It was also a camping stove that provided hot meals and water for teas and coffees. A couple of portable gas heaters which I normally used when I worked in the garage kept us nice and warm, along with an open fire with a back boiler that also provided us with an ample supply of domestic hot water. So was I really that well prepared? Well, if I am brutally honest, no, I was not. It was more by good fortune than good organisation and preparation, but it certainly gave me food for thought, especially as many of my neighbours, some of whom were old and frail, were far less comfortable.

OK, so incidents like this in the UK are fortunately not regular events – but can we assume that that will always be the case? There are some countries that I know of where power cuts are regular events. We have also seen massive powers cuts occurring in the US and Canada. But is the writing on the wall during this age of austerity with the UK's own power supply contingency level dwindling at an alarming rate? In the winter of 2011/12, the UK's spare electricity capacity was over 15% but with the closure of several power stations and others taken offline for maintenance, that figure has now dropped to around four percent (BBC News, 2014). The UK's energy regulator, OFGEM, had warned back in 2012 of an impending crisis which it believed could become critical by 2015 (BBC News, 2012). Recently, I was delivering a business continuity lecture at Manchester Metropolitan University in the UK. I asked the group of around 30 postgraduate students what they would do if they were at home and the lights went out. "Light some candles" said one of them and her response seemed to receive universal agreement. "OK, so how many of you have actually got candles at home?" I asked. Only five or six raised their hands – all were women. I took the discussion onto where are fires most likely to start in the home. "In the kitchen" was the consensus. "So if a pan of fat or oil caught fire, how many of you have a fire extinguisher or fire blanket in the kitchen to stop the fire spreading and possibly the house burning down?" Only two hands showed. "Do you know how to use them?", I enquired, "No" was the response, neither had even given it a thought!

Clearly as a group they were not practising BCM at home, even though common sense warned them of the risks and told them what they needed to do to either mitigate some of the risks they faced, or define some sort of contingency measures. But let us assume that they see the error of their ways and procure some candles and matches, will they be able to find them when they need them? A simple test would of course demonstrate. Turn off the lights and see if you can find the candles and then light them. Moreover, how are you going to ensure they are safe so they don't fall and start a fire, after all, your budget may not stretch to having a convenient candelabra close at hand. One student pointed out, "well that would not be a problem because we all have mobile phones that would help us see what we are doing". That was a fair comment and it was certainly giving encouraging signs that their thinking was heading in the right direction.

What also emerged from our discussions was that none of the students remembered life before the Internet and the launching of the World Wide Web in the mid 1990s. "It's always been there, hasn't it", one of them remarked. None of the students could recall when in 2004 the city of Manchester experienced a massive communication failure because a fire broke out in a tunnel that British Telecom (BT) used to run its network cables. Both primary and backup sets of cables were in the same tunnel and consequently the in-built redundancy that BT had provided was immediately compromised. BT, in its wisdom, had in effect created a massive single point of failure. Over 130,000 BT clients, a combination of business and personal, found themselves without a service, including access to the Internet.

Some shops could not accept debit or credit card payments, withdrawals from some automatic teller machines (ATMs) failed and the emergency services reported that its radio network had become unreliable. Even Manchester Metropolitan University found itself without an Internet service for about seven days. On realising this one student observed, "If this happened again, that means we would have to use the library for our research rather than Google". So that was the contingency sorted out but isn't that what students had to do anyway back in the day. From a professional perspective, I would find no Internet access a massive inconvenience. I know, as I have discovered the hard way. These days I am equipped with several Wi-Fi dongles (for countries I regularly visit) which gives me a degree of peace of mind in this respect.

I moved on to talk about the student's computer arrangements. Some apparently used laptops, some tablets, while others seemed to do everything on their smartphones. "So who backs up their data?" I asked. About half the hands showed. "How do you do it?" Some used the University's file server (a free and sensible option it transpired), a few used the Cloud, others used pen drives and one emailed important files to himself so they were kept on his mail server. The backup frequency varied from daily, to once or twice every 'blue moon'. I then quizzed them about actually checking whether they could recover their data. None had ever tried to, although one argued that was because they had never needed to. Fair comment, or is it? I explained that all my data was backed up to the Cloud which was an ongoing process. It's fantastic, as I don't even need to think about it, as it automatically happens whenever I am connected to the Internet. In all, I estimated that I had close to 200 gigabytes of data in the Cloud.

Then came the day when I dropped my laptop – any one man bands out there that rely on their computers please take note. It didn't bounce. Procuring a replacement PC was relatively straightforward, and as I had a record of all the licences, reloading the software was relatively painless too. But I also needed to urgently reload the data onto the new PC. That is when I discovered that a wireless based recovery from the Cloud would take me the best part of a week or more. I really couldn't wait that long. Fortunately, I also regularly back up my data to an external hard disk which took only minutes to reload. This left me with restoring the most recent Cloud backups which took an hour or so. While it is very dangerous not to back up your data, should you find you cannot recover it quickly enough to meet your needs, I would suggest an alternative strategy may well be in order. All that said, how can you be sure that you can recover your data in a timely fashion if you never actually test that you can?

By raising the profile of practising business continuity at home, it also helps promote the level of awareness in our professional domains by nurturing a culture of being prepared. So ladies and gentlemen, I guess this chapter begs the question that from a BCM perspective, do we practise what we preach in our personal as well as our professional lives? Personally, I would like to think that we preach what we practise.

CHAPTER 4: DEFINING YOUR EXERCISE PROGRAMME

"You can't stop the rain from falling, but you can look for holes in your roof." – Richard Sharpe, 2013

An exercise programme needs to reflect the scope of an organisation's business continuity, while paying due deference to any appropriate legislation and regulations that apply to its industry sector. Its primary objective is to ensure that all aspects of an organisation's BCP have been subjected to an appropriate level of validation. It needs to start simply and gradually increase in complexity as the organisation moves out of its comfort zone, as it prepares to engage in all facets of validating, from simple desk checks to live rehearsals.

The programme will be unique to that organisation and it must be designed to ensure that all information in the plan(s) has been confirmed, the plan(s) has been fully rehearsed, which may also involve the inclusion of suppliers within the activities, and all appropriate employees and their nominated deputies have also been involved in the exercises.

Organisations that choose to adopt the ISO22301 standard will need to apply the Plan-Do-Check-Act model to their exercise programme. An explanation of the model has been included in the following table and is supported by the illustrations in *Figure 9* and *Figure 10*.

Figure 9: Plan/Do/Check/Act model

PLAN (Establish)	Establish business continuity policy, objectives, targets, controls, processes and procedures relevant to improving business continuity, in order to deliver results that align with the organisation's overall policies and objectives.
DO (Implement + operate)	Implement and operate the business continuity policy, controls, processes and procedures.
CHECK (Monitor + review)	Monitor and review performance against business continuity policy and objectives, report the results to management for review, and determine and authorise actions for remediation and improvement.
ACT (Maintain + improve)	Maintain and improve the BCMS by taking corrective action, based on the results of management review and reappraising the scope of the BCMS and business continuity policy and objectives

Figure 10: Plan/Do/Check/Act – explanation
Source: (ISO22301, 2012, p. vi)

As illustrated in *Figure 9*, an exercise programme has four component parts and is a process of continuous improvement. Should you ever get to the end of one programme, you should be ready to start the next. Every exercise needs to be planned, and especially for live rehearsals, I would strongly recommend that organisations undertake a risk assessment. *Figure 11* illustrates the breakdown of the *Execution* module as it is sub-divided into multiple projects. These projects can be exercising or testing any aspect of the BCP, using any one of the various methods (e.g. walkthrough, table top, etc.).

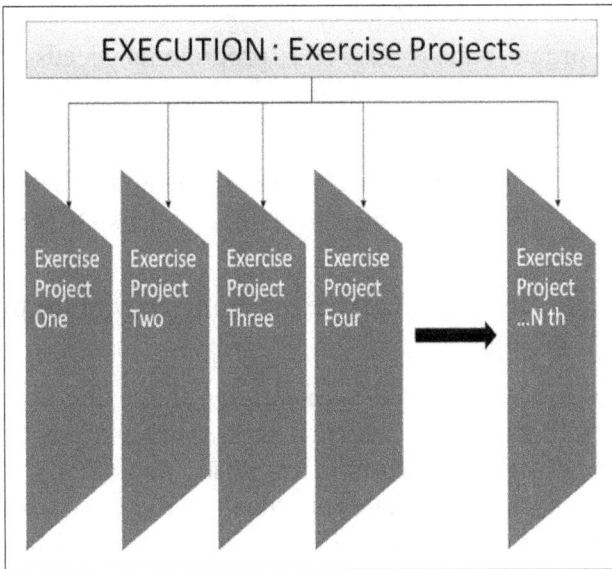

Figure 11: Exercise programme: Execution project relationship

For some large organisations, the exercise programme could run for several years before it completes a cycle. Typically, it will encompass a series of exercise projects, each of which, while contributing to the overall programme objectives, will have its own set of objectives and deliverables. As *Figure 11* illustrates, the ratio of an exercise programme to a project is one to many. The example shows the programme starting from 'Project One' and running through to the 'Nth Project'.

Depending on the level of importance attached to specific projects, some may be run once over the lifetime of a programme, while others may be run regularly. For example, I know of several organisations that regularly test that their generators will automatically trigger when isolated from the power.

Every organisation's exercise programme needs to be regularly reviewed, especially if it is expected to run over several years:

* Does it still meet the objectives, keeping in mind an organisation will change over time and its BCMS must remain in step?
* Does it continue to validate the proficiency of the overall BCM programme?

You must never make the assumption that some aspect of your BCP will work and use this as an excuse for not subjecting it to some form of exercise. You simply cannot consider it to be reliable until it has been exercised, regardless of how much effort or attention to detail was spent on creating the related strategies or building the BCP itself. An exercise will invariably always find something that needs to be modified, however small.

The process is looking to assess an organisation's business continuity level of competence, while identifying areas for improvement. It should also be capable of flagging missing information – even something simple like a telephone number. Moreover, it should emphasise where assumptions have been made and especially those that may need to be questioned. Any assumption that has not been verified, should be considered to be a risk. Of course one key area that an exercise must address is that of does the BCP enable an interrupted business to be effectively restored within the time parameters, the recovery time objectives, as specified in the BIA?

Any organisation that is new to BCP validation needs to remember the expression – 'learn to walk before you try and run'. If you have just completed your first BCP, do not, for example, decide to start out by:

• trying to exercise your entire BCP in one tranche, or

• opt to make your first exercise a 'live' rehearsal.

Both would be extremely unwise decisions. Exercises should start out as simple undertakings and gradually increase in their complexity and challenge. But all that said, an organisation needs to be careful not to make the scope of its exercises too narrow, while keeping the level of complexity low, as this will not stretch the recovery teams, while potentially constraining their development and confidence levels. Exercises need to be able to help foster confidence in its participants while encouraging a maturing sense of team work. Exercise should also be used to take every opportunity of raising the level of awareness of business continuity throughout an organisation.

Technique	Desired Outcome
Technical	Does all the necessary equipment function (e.g. generators, backup servers, desktops, telephony, etc.)?
Procedural	Are all the plans and procedures correct?
Logical	Do the procedures logically function together?
Timeliness	Can the procedures achieve the essential recovery time objective (RTO) for each activity? Moreover, can multiple RTOs be met in a worst case scenario?
Administrative	Are all the procedures practical?
Ratify	Do all the contingency arrangements work?
Personnel	Have the right people, including suppliers' staff, been allocated to incident response duties? Do these team members have the prerequisite skills and experience? Are team members familiar with their roles?

Figure 12: Exercise programme techniques

Figure 12 provides some examples of the techniques that the exercise programme has at its disposal, and which should be appropriately utilised to ensure that the objectives are achieved across the whole organisation over a pre-defined timetable. Exercises that show serious deficiencies or inaccuracies in the procedures should be rerun after corrective actions have been completed.

Naturally, along with the duration of an exercise programme, the frequency of exercising is very much influenced by the very character of the organisation's business and its size. When compared to a large international corporation, your average SME is small by definition, and is very likely to have a somewhat simple product base and structure. Regardless of organisational size comparisons, the greater the frequency that the incident response team members are involved in exercises, the more proficient they will become. Even so, it is recommended that the exercise programme safeguards business continuity validation integrity by insisting that every member of an organisation's incident response team, along with their deputies, should be involved in an exercise at least annually.

Those organisations that have embraced the BCM lifecycle as the holistic process it was designed to be, will be able to refer to their business continuity policy statements and BCM programme management, and derive direction on how the exercise programme is to be planned and managed. Training needs analysis will also assist in identifying requirements for any specialist training needed by the incident response team candidates.

> *"An exercise is a process to train for, assess, practice and improve performance in an organisation."* (Jacque, 2010, p. 4)

> *"Exercising is a generic phrase used in the GPG that encompasses 'testing' which is a unique form of exercise with a pass or fail element, commonly utilised when testing equipment or technology. Exercises are used for validating policy, plans, training, communications, and for rehearsing the roles and responsibilities of teams and individuals."* (BCI, 2013, p. 95)

> *"An exercise can be many different things but all of them have the objective of exploring how your business continuity arrangements will stand up to the pressure of real events. An exercise needs to be a learning event that tells you about areas of strength and weakness."* (Sterling, et al., 2012, p. 170)

Here we have three variations of the definition of an exercise. Even so, the common theme that stands out is learning and training.

4.1 Securing an exercise programme budget

"At the time of disaster, no one complains about the Business Continuity budget!" – Don Hill

Thinking back to my days of disaster recovery fall-back tests at IBM in the 1970s and 1980s, I am sure there must have been a budget assigned, although that was a side of things I was not involved with during my time with 'Big Blue'. I just got on with whatever roles and responsibilities that I was assigned to do for each of the DR tests I was involved with. But any reality check will insist on an agreed budget being in place. So when it comes down to defining your exercise programme, the budget will more often than not have a constraining effect on what you can and cannot expect to achieve. It will invariably have a direct influence on how long you can assume the programme will run for, and you can usually anticipate that it can be measured in years for larger organisations.

So the exercise programme planner's first dilemma could simply be "Do I define a programme and then seek budget approval or do I find out how much is in the budget and work from there?"

However, before trying to solve this dilemma or commencing work on your first draft, it is often well worth discussing the exercise programme with senior management. They may perceive specific weaknesses that they would like to see given some sort of priority, or they could have a specific fear that maybe keeps them awake at night. Their collective thoughts may well help to shape the direction that the programme ultimately takes and it could well influence the size of the budget too. For example, one CIO I recently spoke to told me that the cyber threat had evolved into a growing and menacing nightmare for him. Extensive exercises in this arena would certainly get his vote.

Even so, be prepared to work without any specific input from the senior management team. Before this meeting with them, do your own preparation too. Do not go to them with a blank sheet of paper and expect them to fill it in for you. Many managers expect their employees to go to them with solutions rather than problems, and perhaps present them with options and recommendations. In these situations the managers will 'pay their money and make their choice'.

As part of your preparation, you will need to consider how experienced your organisation is in matters relating to BCM, and specifically with respect to exercising. If it is new to the game, then whatever you include within the programme plan, keep it simple but be prepared to defend its simplicity if management expectations demand a greater degree of exercising complexity. The scope of your BCM will help define the options you have in what you should consider including in the programme. Do not forget that the scope of your BCM may not include the entire organisation.

For a more experienced organisation, look for ways to stretch the incident teams assigned to the exercises. Remember to factor in any training requirements that have been identified for the participants. Review your past results and look for any activity that has not been exercised recently, or exercises where there were lessons that needed to be learned – have they in fact been learned!

Both the inexperienced and experienced organisation will need to take account of what resources will be required, and verify that they are available when needed. Keep in mind that, ideally, those individuals who have been given some form of role within the incident management arena will also require a nominated deputy. These deputies will also need to be exercised too. You will also need to check that whatever facilities you need (e.g. specific meeting rooms and equipment, etc.) are available.

Section 4.2.1 describes the types of exercise that you should consider using including the 'pass' or 'fail' testing approach, usually the domain of all things technical. You are now ready to begin constructing the plan for your exercise programme. Treat each exercise as a separate project within the programme (see page 62) and even though you may expect the overall programme to run for several years, do not try and create a plan to encompass the entire duration. Break it down into bite size chunks of possibly 12 months each. You can even create a rolling plan which, when one month has been completed, you consider what to include in the corresponding month for next year.

Finally, when your exercise programme plan is ready, present it to senior management for approval.

4.2 Planning your exercises

"Business continuity testing can be complex and this could explain why only 30% of companies actually test their plans. Many fear that it will be costly and difficult to do." (Varley, 2010)

I have always felt that a computer programmer is someone who ideally needs to have a logical and creative streak in their psyche, whereas a software tester needs to have a destructive inclination. The latter is, after all, trying to methodically break what the programmer has created. As for business continuity managers, they need to be more flexible and versatile. When you consider what is expected of them by the BCM lifecycle, it stands to reason that they need to be creative with the strategy design and BCP implementation phases but then destructive when dealing with validation.

> *"There is no limit to the imagination of the business continuity manager when it comes to exercising."* (Armit, 2007, p. 324)

An interesting thought from Armit but one of the first rules of planning your exercises and tests is that they need to be realistic. Getting the objectives right is a key part of the exercise planning process and its importance should not be underestimated. Failure to observe this golden rule could result in the exercise becoming unmanageable, fragmented and attenuated. Every exercise should have a set of objectives that are:

- **Precise** and to the point (no waffle or unnecessary rhetoric).

- **Measurable** with clearly defined key performance indicators, along with an appropriate set of critical success factors.

- **Achievable** and not too optimistic in terms of what can be accomplished within the allotted timescales.

- **Realistic** and not trying to plan exercises for scenarios that are highly unlikely to happen.

- **Targeting** specific aspects of a BCP may allow you to invite subject matter experts to support exercises, whereas a broader scope may make it far less cost beneficial for them to attend.

To reiterate the point of making the exercise convincing, if the BCM manager proposes an exercise where the scenario features a hurricane in a country that is not prone to visits from these highly destructive natural phenomena, they may not be taken very seriously and their credibility could suffer as a consequence.

The list of what needs to be considered for inclusion in the exercise programme for some organisations may be extensive but could include examples, such as:

- Scenario exercises (e.g. denial of access, pandemic, terrorist attack, flooding, utility failure, cyber attack, etc.)
- Component testing (e.g. standby generators, etc.)
- Business contingency exercises (e.g. can a bank's branch staff continue to process deposits and withdrawals when there has been an ICT failure, etc.?)
- ICT disaster recovery exercises
- Media exercising for face to face sessions with newspaper, radio and television journalists, in addition to managing the demands of social media
- Call tree cascade exercise
- Supplier failure (e.g. bankruptcy, the suppliers suffer a serious incident, does 24/7 support mean 24/7?, etc.)

Remember, an exercise is a project and familiarity with a project management process (e.g. PRINCE2 or Agile, etc.), along with planning tools, such as Microsoft Project, will certainly help. If your organisation has already adopted a particular methodology, then it would seem appropriate to use that rather than go in search of an alternative. However, regretfully, it is not possible to include guidance on project management in this book but for those of you not well versed in the ways of project management, I would recommend at least learning the basics.

Firstly, your exercise project will need to be aligned with the exercise programme, unless the deviation is sanctioned by management for some other reason. For those organisations that do not run a 24 hour operation, ideally, some exercises should be conducted during normal business hours while some should be outside. It is worth remembering that if your working day is less than 12 hours, there is a greater likelihood that an incident could occur outside of normal business hours.

When selecting a date for the exercise, if at all possible, be careful to avoid public holidays, religious holidays, Valentine's Day, Mother's Day and Father's Day, as staff may well already have other plans. If you are planning a weekend exercise, to avoid any confusion it may well be worth avoiding the day clocks change from winter to summertime or vice versa. A commonly-accepted approach is to select the dates where the required resources available are at maximum, while the business loads or transactions are minimal.

The plan will need to define a number of key points including:

- Selected method of exercise (please refer to *Figure 13: Choosing a method of exercise*).
- What is the purpose and the aims of the exercise?
- Describe the exercise/scenario including the scope.

Qualities		Method of exercise					
		Drill	Seminar	Table-top	Simulation	Live	
Ease of creation	(1 = Easy)	1–3	2–4	3–6	4–8	4–10	(10 = Hard)
Development time	(1 = Quick)	1–2	2–4	3–6	4–8	5–10	(10 = Lengthy)
Cost	(1 = Cheap)	1–4	2–4	2–5	3–7	4–10	(10 = Expensive)
Level of corporate risk	(1 = Low risk)	1–3	1–2	1–3	3–6	5–10	(10 = High risk)
Numbers of players who can take part	(1= Few)	1–5	1–7	2–6	2–6	1–10	(10 = Many)
Pressure generated on players	(1 = Little pressure)	1	1	3–7	3–8	5–10	(10 = High pressure)
Amount of realism that can be generated	(1 = Limited realism)	1–3	1–2	2–4	3–7	8–10	(10 = Almost the real thing)
Numbers of directing staff needed	(1 = Few)	1–3	1–2	1–2	4–8	5–10	(10 = Many)
Method of developing plans	(1 = Not a good method)	1–2	4–8	3–7	1–3	1–3	(10 = Excellent method)
Way of evaluating plans	(1 = Not a good method)	2–4	1–3	2–5	2–8	7–10	(10 = Excellent method)

Figure 13: Choosing a method of exercise
Source: (BSI, 2010)

- Measurable objectives and intangible objectives.

- Define the desired outcomes.

- Risk assessment report specifically for the validation activity, but especially for live exercises, which could include financial, resource or time constraints.

- The venue or venues where the exercise will be held. Keep in mind that separate break-out rooms can often be useful.

- Non people resources (e.g. conference phone, television, overhead project and screen, pens, paper, etc.).

- Timetable/project plan detailing what is happening before, during and after the exercise. Do not forget to allow time in the plan for breaks.

- Exercise duration plus simulated duration.

- Who will be involved in the exercise, not forgetting resource requirements which are external to the organisation (e.g. suppliers, emergency services, etc.).

- Incident management team(s) – strategic, tactical and operational, as appropriate.
- Estimates of effort required from each participant (e.g. in hours, days, etc.).
- Facilitator, observer, record keeper (sometimes called 'the scribe'), as appropriate.
- Any other interested parties – such as auditors.
- Debrief arrangements (hot – immediately after exercise, followed by a cold exercise, perhaps a week or two after the exercise conclusion).
- Preparation and publication of exercise report, along with a proposed timetable to address any ensuing action plans.

The plan will need to be supported with an appropriate exercise timeline accompanied by a script, briefing documentation, injects and supporting media material.

There will be some organisations that should prepare and exercise their business continuity plans in conjunction with other parties. Moreover, resources could be required from suppliers, emergency services, local authorities or regulators. It is quite possible that expertise may be required that does not exist within your organisation, such as a cyber security specialist. Involving these external resources in the actual exercise planning stage makes sense, as they will invariably be experts in their own right and should be able to make a worthwhile contribution to the process.

To combat the danger of some form of implied direction being included in plans, I have come across a couple of organisations who have temporarily brought in outside specialists who have no prior involvement with those organisations, with the purpose of using their expertise to validate plans. For example, a database whizz-kid or a desktop PC guru might be brought in to walk through the plans for database or desktop environment recovery. They will have no proprietary knowledge in their heads, so the only thing they will have to work with is their experience and what has been included in the plan.

As part of your preparation, do not overlook administrative issues, as a lack of attention to detail can have a negative effect on the proceedings. I consider the provision of refreshments to be essential. A good supply of bottled water plus tea and coffee can certainly help 'oil the wheels'. If time is tight, it can also be worth stretching the budget to include a buffet to allow for a working lunch.

4.2.1 Types of exercise

You will have noted that *Figure 7: Evolution of GPG exercise terminology* illustrates that there have been many different names given to the various different types of approach that can be adopted to exercise your BCP. Invariably, each name can generally be associated with a level of simplicity or complexity. This section will reference the 2013 edition of the BCI's GPG which defines the following five categories:

1. Discussion based exercises
2. Table top exercises
3. Command post exercises
4. Live
5. Test.

With the exception of a 'Test' which is invariably a pass or fail exercise (e.g. Did the generator automatically start when disconnected from the power? – Yes/No, etc.), ideally every exercise should be designed to be a 'no-fault' learning experience.

4.2.1.1 Discussion based exercises

While the BCI GPG identifies the discussion based approach as a low risk but highly cost effective means of exercising, it does not provide any significant details with regard to specific examples of how discussion exercises would be expected to operate. However, here, ISO22398 can help, as it breaks the discussion based approach into four component parts:

1. Seminar
2. Workshop
3. Table top exercise
4. Discussion based game.

You will note that while the GPG includes the table top exercises as its second level of exercise, ISO22398 includes it as an integral part of the level one discussion based level exercising.

I have personally used each of the four ISO22398 listed approaches, although in hindsight, I feel that my experience of the seminar method was more focused on awareness training than conducting a specific exercise. While each has a part to play, I particularly like the workshop approach. In my view it is low risk and relatively inexpensive but it is an effective method that allows the flexibility of complexity variation as desired.

A comparative newcomer to the exercise scene is the discussion based game and there are some proprietary based examples that have been reported in the media.

Personally, I have only used the Business Continuity Institute's BC24 incident simulation game. Launched in 2011, *"BC24 provides an excellent tool to support the embedding of Business Continuity (BC) across an organisation and its partners and can form an essential part of developing a resilience capability through exercising."* (BCI, 2015).

Category	Method	Description
Discussions	Seminar	An informal discussion method, assisted by an experienced facilitator, designed to orient participants to new or updated plans, policies or procedures unconstrained by real-time simulation of events. May be used by organisations as an initial organising point when plans and programmes are being revised or developed, for example, to review and revise a procedure that proved difficult to implement during a recent actual disruptive event.
	Workshop	Similar to seminars but differ as participant interaction is increased, and the focus is on achieving or building a product, such as new standard operating procedures, emergency operations plans, multi-year plans, or improvement plans. Workshops are often employed during exercise development to write exercise performance objectives and scenarios.
	Table top exercise	Includes key personnel who discuss simulated scenarios in an informal setting and used as a tool to build competence and support for a revised plan or procedure, or review plans, policies, and procedures and to assess the processes and systems needed to respond to undesired situations. Issues that result from the simulated events are

		discussed by the participants who develop decisions through paced problem solving. They can be timed to require rapid decision making or untimed allowing for in depth discussion and development of solutions. Untimed table top exercises are commonly used first and timed exercises second.
	Discussion based game	A simulation of operations often involving two or more teams in a competitive environment, using rules, data and procedures designed to depict an actual or assumed real-life situation. Gaming and simulation are often discussion-based. Games are also called 'virtual exercises' and use technology to engage participants and create stress through the simulation of behavioural conditions.

Figure 14: ISO22398 Discussion based exercise definitions
Source: (ISO22398, 2012, p. 17)

4.2.1.2 Walkthrough

Although this is not listed in Section 4.2.1, I intentionally mention the walkthrough as it was featured as a type of exercising option up to and including the 2010 edition of the GPG. Accordingly, it was less than two years ago that the name was dropped, when the 2013 edition of the GPG was launched. Therefore, you may occasionally come across the expression 'walkthrough' which could still be used, in a comparable way to the 'exercise' versus 'test' argument that I mentioned in 'Section 2.1 – What's in a name?'. Similarly, it is probably the force of habit that keeps it to the fore.

The nearest replacement to the walkthrough in the 2013 edition of the GPG was the table top exercise which is covered in the following section.

4.2.1.3 Table top exercises

A table top exercise is a very powerful and flexible low risk approach in the validation tool box. It can be both cost effective and realistic. However, at the outset, it must be appreciated that it is not intended to create a 'pass' or 'fail' end result, that is the domain of Section 4.2.1.6 – 'Test' on page 76. Moreover, it should not be used to assess individuals but should be aimed primarily at proving that the plan is complete and fit for purpose. That said, any learning opportunities that present themselves for participants should be maximised.

All participants must be familiar with the plans being exercised, along with their particular roles and responsibilities, although they may not have been briefed beforehand on the actual scenario that will be played out. I have stopped exercises when it became apparent that a lack of preparation by some participants was proving to be to the severe detriment of the exercise. In other words, it was wasting the time of those who were ready.

Management must be prepared to commit theirs and their staffs' availability to the exercise, as there can be nothing more disruptive than a team member being dragged out of an exercise, particularly if they do not come back. If interruptions prove to be a problem, it is even worth considering holding the exercise away from the organisation's premises, perhaps in a suitable hotel's business suite.

In my opinion, one of life's modern enigmas is the mobile phone. On the one hand it has given us the amazing ability to be able to contact people at any time and almost anywhere on the planet. We can interact with the Internet day or night, making full use of the ever growing plethora of Apps that are available. Conversely, some people seem to be permanently 'joined at the hip' to their mobile phones and their lives appear to be totally ruled by the need for some form of addictive and continuous interaction. The sad fact is that the side effect of mobile phones is that they can also be an immense source of distraction and disruption. So let me say something potentially contentious. My recommendation is to ban mobile phones unless they are an absolutely essential part of the exercise!

> *"A major flaw that I see in table-top exercises is that people often state what they 'would' do without ever determining the feasibility of that decision. What would be more constructive is that if during a table-top exercise there is a rule that when a person states they 'would' do something, they demonstrate that it is hypothetically feasible rather than simply an aspiration. They should be required to explain both how and why they would take the stated action."* (Abide, 2013)

The table top can also be used to take account of whether a suitable level of enabling infrastructure is in place to satisfy those plans. As part of the overall exercise programme objectives, visible management buy-in is essential, ideally from the board member who is sponsoring the BCMS. The significance of the importance of what exercising is aiming to achieve cannot be understated and it could not be impressed upon participants more than if the sponsor opens the proceedings by addressing the team. Equally, if several managers and even board members are seen by employees to be attending an exercise, it should act as a demonstration of how seriously BCM is being taken by the upper echelons of the organisation.

While it may focus on a pre-determined scenario, the potential benefits and outcomes from the table top exercise are substantial. It can be used to identify whether:

- the plan is realistic and meets all the recovery requirements
- appropriate links between inter-plan dependencies have been correctly defined, while providing an effective handshake between plans
- all the assumptions made within the plan have been validated and are correct
- all the expectations of the various disparate business and support areas are realistic and accurate
- both managerial and support roles and responsibilities within the plan are clearly defined and fully understood by the respective employees assigned to them. This includes all levels of management, up to and including board level
- endeavour to make all walkthroughs high visibility events throughout the organisation, as this will create an enormous chance to accentuate the importance of business continuity.

In executing a table top exercise, the script or scenario allows for using either a 'real time' situation, or the simulation of extended periods where, for example, a scenario with a three day elapsed time by using 'time jumps', can be consolidated into a seven hour exercise.

The table top exercise can bring disparate groups together, such as internal service providers (e.g. ICT, building facilities management and human resources, etc.), along with representation from the various business units. It provides an excellent opportunity to examine everyone else's opinions and assumptions which can be found to contradict each other. However, on one such occasion, a very defensive ICT manager totally missed the point of the exercise and took it personally when questioned over his team's ability to respond to multiple scenarios. Having already made the statement that ICT could recover any one of the mission critical systems within their respective recovery time objectives (RTO), he was asked could they meet the RTOs if they had to manage a simultaneous recovery of several systems. It transpired that resourcing constraints meant that the answer was 'No' and he took the question as an implied criticism. However, on a positive note, the exercise had teased out this potentially serious exposure but also the message to always ensure that participants know exactly why they are there and what is expected of them.

On completion of the table top exercise, a debriefing session must be held (please refer to section 4.4). All findings, conclusions and recommendations need to be fully documented and presented to senior management, along with an action plan that stipulates what additions, modifications and deletions are required to the BCMS.

4.2.1.4 Command post exercises

Command post exercises would generally be expected to provide an opportunity to involve every level of an organisation's response capability. A large organisation will probably have set up a strategic, tactical and operational level of incident response. Conversely, a small organisation may only be able to justify one level. In fact, it may have insufficient employees, making more than one level a gross overkill. In micro organisations, it is entirely possible that

CEOs not only manage a crisis but also have to roll up their sleeves and fix it too.

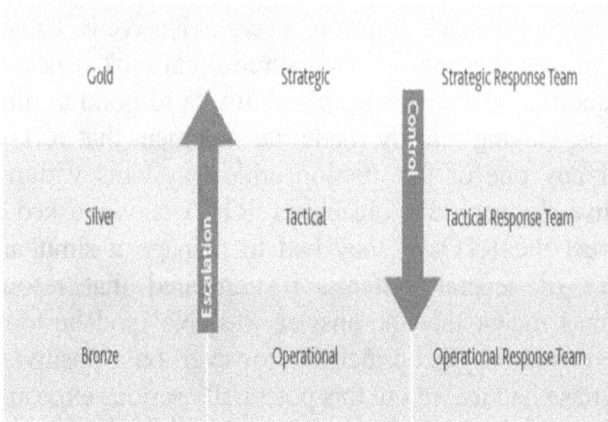

Figure 15: Three tier incident response structure
Source: (BCI, 2010, p. 69)

Sometimes referred to as the Gold, Silver and Bronze levels of incident response, *Figure 15* illustrates the flow of actions with 'escalation' ascending the chain of command and 'control' descending.

Again, this level of exercise is more expensive than its predecessors, due to the inevitable involvement of more resources including senior management. However, as this is still not dealing with a live situation, the risk of disruption would not generally be high. These exercises, depending on the selected scenarios, could demand the involvement of employees from right across an organisation, or just discrete parts of an organisation. They can be held with participants working from their normal place of work, as in the case study described in section 6.4, although some scenarios, such as denial of access, would usually derive added benefit if acted out remotely from the workplace. My own personal experience has been that by working remotely, participants are less likely to be interrupted by the demands of the 'day job' which can of course be disruptive to the overall exercise.

Consideration needs to be given to the setting up of an incident management room or crisis management suite, as it is sometimes referred. To allow the participants to develop familiarity with an incident management room that would be used in dealing with a real incident, using these facilities during an exercise can only help. Among the most impressive I have seen were two that were set up in the UK by local authorities in order to meet the criterion and expectations of the Civil Contingencies Act 2004. These were standalone, dedicated suites of rooms that were fully equipped to deal with civil emergencies, such as the 2007 Gloucestershire floods.

"The 2007 floods in Britain resulted in the largest civil emergency response since World War II."
(Dakin, 2014, p. 183)

Both these local authorities had access to alternative facilities in case their primary crisis management suites were a consequential loss of the emergency they were facing.

However, for some organisations, this would be a luxury that just could not be justified. Even so, the room, or suite of rooms, needs to be comfortable and fitted out with some bare essentials that should either be permanently in situ or readily available to set up an incident management room:

- Tables and chairs which needs to take account of the maximum number of participants who will need to be accommodated in the incident management room. This should be derived from the roles and responsibilities that were defined during the creation of the business continuity plan.

- Telephones (landline and mobiles) including conference call facilities. However, keep in mind that these need to be effective enough for the call recipient to be able to hear everyone on the call. Not all conference call telephone sets are good enough to meet this requirement.
- For a multi-site operation, a video conference link may prove invaluable.
- Television (to monitor the news media for the status of external events, such as floods, terrorism, chemical release, etc.).
- Internet connectivity – ideally both Wifi and Ethernet.
- Desktop/laptop ICT capability which is Internet enabled.
- Stationery – pens, paper and Post-its®.
- Flip chart holders with ample supply of flip chart paper and marker pens.
- White boards.
- Screen and projector can also be useful for status reporting.
- Audio/video recording equipment which could be invaluable during post exercise reviews.

The scenarios selected should provide participants with situations that are realistic, using information that is as close as possible to what could be anticipated in a real incident. They should also provide the means of assessing the decision-making process and information flow, plus the efficiency of the BCP and related procedures. Effective communications are critical. In the case study considered in Section 6.1, the exercise was primarily about validating the ability to communicate in a denial of access situation with over 50 independent organisations participating. However, whatever the scenario, participants also need to be mindful of the effectiveness and efficiency of the incident management room configuration including the equipment.

4.2.1.5 Live exercises

Now with live exercising in mind, let us start with the warning that these activities are usually high risk and expensive to run. The pre-set objectives will generally be more complex than just a simple binary 'Yes' it worked or 'No' it did not. In fact, business continuity professionals should invariably try and avoid a 'pass' or 'fail' outcome from an exercise. The binary test will be covered in Section 4.2.1.6. Moreover, ICT disaster recovery, including live cutover testing, has been included in section 5.2.

For some full scale live exercises, the resources required could be significant, resulting in lost production while placing a financial burden on the exercise programme's budget. Of the range of exercise types available, this is likely to be the one least used and, for organisations new to BCM, the type of exercise that it would be very unwise to start with. In the event of something going wrong in a live exercise, some scenarios may have the potential to actually have a damaging effect on your organisation's ability to operate, placing its reputation and possibly even its very survival in jeopardy. Insurers may even choose to wash their hands of your organisation if it tries to claim against a self-inflicted disaster.

However, please do not let this warning deter you from including live exercises in your programme. They do have an important part to play. For much of my 15 years at IBM, the majority of the exercises I was involved with were primarily live. That said, even back in the 1970s, IBM's appreciation and experience of what passed for business continuity in those days was very advanced.

The scale of a live exercise is flexible. That is to say that you can select a discrete part of the organisation to exercise, or the entire operation. Sections 6.4 and 6.5 are both examples of case studies where only parts of the respective organisations were chosen to be validated. These exercises would normally be expected to involve anyone who would be required to support a response. However, in certain cases (see Section 6.4) the incident selected was a multi-faceted scenario and one aspect of it assumed both injuries and fatalities had occurred amongst the employees. As these 'unfortunate' individuals were selected at random, it transpired that some were actually considered vital to the success of the recovery. This gave the organisation the chance to prove that no one is indispensable!

But even a live rehearsal can start off gently and with a very narrow risk, cost and scope base. For example, if an employee is designated to work from home during an incident, can he/she actually do that? If a business unit is being relocated in the event of a denial of access, can the alternative premises be made ready within the agreed timescales and is all the functionality and equipment they require working correctly? The exercising of a building's evacuation procedure is something that every occupant in that building would be expected to participate in. In fact, the introductory example in *Chapter 1* was focusing on such an instance. You may even consider whether you wish to invite the emergency services to participate, to add some extra realism. In the case study considered in section 7.2, it was decided not to involve the Fire and Rescue Service but they turned up anyway.

It is not unusual for various organisations to have to initiate an exercise where they have to work together. Section 6.1

looks at the case when the Hong Kong financial regulator ran an exercise involving 55 local banks and financial institutions. As it transpired, the exercise was well timed, as the scenario selected actually became a reality just a few months later.

It can be difficult, if not impossible, to re-create the stress and anxiety that could be expected to be generated in a real event, especially if the scenario selected is potentially life threatening. It was a paramedic who attended victims from the 2013 Boston Marathon bombing that said that none of their extensive training could have prepared them for what they had to deal with that day. Section 6.2 carries two examples of making the situation as close to reality as possible. Section 6.3 continues the theme and in this case study volunteers masquerading as victims were briefed on how to behave to maximise the realism for the participants.

My research has come across numerous cases of employees working around the clock in response to real incidents. Perhaps expecting or achieving this level of commitment during an exercise is unusual, although sometimes the nature of an organisation's business may demand that live exercises are only conducted outside of normal business hours. However, in one exercise that demanded more than a round the clock involvement from its participants:

> *"Some key personnel worked for up to 38 hours, at which stage they were making mistakes and showing signs of tiredness. However, this is what would happen in reality and as such must be addressed through testing."* (Armit, 2007, p. 336)

Armit makes a valuable point and I can certainly recall a number of occasions of having to work round the clock when a serious incident occurred. If an unresolved problem is allowed to deteriorate and threaten the very survival of an organisation, should the recovery team decide to insist upon working a normal nine to five day it would be tantamount to turkeys voting for Thanksgiving or Christmas!

We must not forget that live exercises are an ideal way to train employees including those who would probably not be considered as part of an incident management team. Even knowing what to do and how to behave in an evacuation is a basic part of that training.

Attention to detail is crucial when planning a live exercise, along with performing an effective risk assessment that considers 'What could possibly go wrong?'. The resources required, which could include suppliers and even clients, could be substantial and costly. Particular caution should also be applied to the avoidance of any disruption to business as usual activities. Before commencing, management must be clearly appraised of all aspects of the exercise, as they should ultimately have the final word on a 'Go' or 'No Go' decision.

4.2.1.6 Testing

Compared with other exercises, testing is unique insofar as the outcome has a 'pass' or 'fail' expectation. It would normally relate to equipment, recovery procedures or technology. However, when dealing with people, an examination type situation should be avoided in favour of a learning experience.

Some appropriate tests might include:

- Can a server be procured, commissioned and be ready for use within a pre-set recovery time objective (RTO)?
- Alternatively, can data be retrieved from an organisation's vital record's store and be restored within the RTO?

- Can a call tree cascade be completed within a pre-determined timescale?
- Can a building be safely evacuated within a target timeframe?

4.3 Executing your exercises

"All sorts of good reasons are given for postponing an exercise, from the understandable fact that everyone is just too busy at the present time to the ludicrous idea that the recovery shouldn't be exercised until it is known to work (which came first, the chicken or the egg?) And so it goes on, month after month, year after year, with everyone saying that they intend to run an exercise, but with nobody committing to a date or time." (The Business Continuity Consultant, 2015)

The exercise can be either announced or unannounced and case studies of both have been included in *Chapter 6*. Either way, it is important that participants are made aware that it is an exercise. For example, four days after the terrorist attacks in Sousse, Tunisia, Lyon, France and Kuwait on 26 June 2015, first responders were rehearsing for a terrorist attack in London. This was not a response to the events that had occurred four days earlier and in fact planning for the exercise had been six months in the making. Moreover, the authorities went to great lengths to ensure that the event was publicised for what it was – a training exercise.

The name of every attendee should be recorded – it is quite possible that who was expected and who actually came will differ. They will need to be fully briefed and aware of:

- the exercise scenario and objectives and how the latter will be measured

- their role and responsibilities
- where participants do not know each other, introductions would be appropriate – who are they, why are they involved in the exercise and their area of expertise
- how the exercise will be conducted. They need to appreciate that it is part of a continuous improvement programme for business continuity and that it is certainly not intended to apportion blame
- the estimated end time
- post exercise activities.

For an announced exercise, briefing materials can be circulated prior to the event. For an unannounced exercise, time will need to be built into the timeline to allow for this preparation. Triggering the start of the exercise should be predefined. For the case study in Section 6.5, activating the fire alarm was the selected criteria although an inject can be used just as well, as has been demonstrated in Section 6.7.

In my view, the unsung heroes that attend these events are the scribes. The importance of their role in documenting what happens cannot be understated. If they are new to this role, it is certainly worth investing some time in making sure they understand exactly what is expected of them. If you also have a good example of what has been recorded in a previous exercise, it would be worth sharing this with them as part of their learning curve. Some organisations choose to use audio or video equipment to record the proceedings instead of appointing a scribe – personally I would opt for both. Even with the availability of voice recognition software, without a scribe present someone will still need to ensure that an accurate record is available.

An exercise may be suspended or terminated before the scheduled time, for one of a number of reasons including:

- A genuine incident has occurred
- The exercise has achieved its objectives
- A time-chop has to be used as the exercise has overrun[2]
- It has become clear that little more can be achieved
- The health and safety of participants is threatened.

A few of the events I have been involved with have been complex and were scheduled to run all weekend. In one case, it was run over the Easter holiday weekend which in the UK lasts for four days. During these extended sessions, a series of checkpoints were always built into the plan with Go/No-Go decisions that had to be made before we moved onto the next phase. We always had back-out plans in place, so if necessary the '*status quo*' could be restored at any time. One of these exercises in which ICT were heavily involved had to be abandoned after lightning struck the building housing the data centre and all the mainframe computers freaked-out and immediately powered off. So we went from exercise into a genuine crisis management mode in the space of a few seconds.

Unexpected opportunities can present themselves during exercises when it may be worth taking a time out. For instance, something may generate discussion points that, even though it may be perhaps a deviation from the exercise, have the potential to facilitate an unexpected learning experience. Try and avoid dismissing these

---

[2] Following an over-running exercise, I once found myself locked in a client site as my visitor's pass would not allow me to go through the unmanned security gates after 7 pm.

openings solely in the interest of sticking to the intended timetable.

During an exercise, it is possible that a great deal of material can be produced. This should all be collected up at the end – even notes scribbled by participants. If audio, video or photographic records are created, they should also be saved and used as input to the post exercise report.

4.4 Post exercise activity

The post exercise activity comes in three parts:

1. A short hot debrief which should immediately follow the end of the exercise, when recollections of what happened are still fresh in the minds of the participants.
2. The cold debrief which follows a week or two after the exercise.
3. Report writing which will include conclusions and recommendations.

Like the exercise, both debriefing sessions should have a scribe in attendance to record the proceedings.

4.4.1 Hot debrief

The exercise timeline should include a slot to hold a hot debrief before the participants disperse. This is intended to capture the participant's thoughts and feedback, regardless of how senior or junior their organisational status happens to be. Either way, the debrief chairperson should ensure that everyone has the opportunity to be heard.

You will be looking to capture their honest opinions on the key issues that arose. You may need to steer the meeting clear of any temptation that may exist to regurgitate what has already been said or done, as this should have been captured during the event itself. After a stressful exercise session, people can be tense, and a tight control of the meeting may be essential to avoid a free for all, especially if any contentious issues are raised. It is certainly worth considering any discrepancies that could have occurred between what was in the plan, what actually happened, and the reasons for the differences. Certainly look to identify:

- What went well
- What could have been done better, and
- What went badly
- Lessons learned
- Did the exercise reveal any risks or issues that need further consideration?

If anyone feels the need to criticise, then you need to encourage them to make their criticism constructive rather than destructive. You want them to think and reflect plus give you their opinions and feelings, so try and avoid closed questions. While you are not trying to lead the witness, instead nurture them by asking questions, such as *"So what would you have done?"*, *"How would you have approached that particular issue?"*, *"What improvements do you feel we could have added?"* or *"How would you feel if we did this instead?"*, etc.

Any aspiring debriefing session chairpersons/facilitators could do a lot worse than watch the award-winning training films produced by John Cleese entitled "Meetings, bloody meetings" and its sequel "More bloody meetings". In these productions, Cleese delivers some very serious messages about preparing for and running meetings but in a very humorous way. However, there are some extremely beneficial lessons to be learned that would be invaluable in a debrief situation.

4.4.2 Cold debrief

Normally held a week or two after the exercise, this debriefing session is intended to take a more in-depth look at the event. However, organising a cold debrief can prove somewhat difficult, insofar as all the exercise attendees have dispersed and it may prove logistically challenging to re-assemble them simultaneously. This will be especially true if the exercise was a multi-agency affair. Try and combat this by ensuring that the date and venue for the debriefing has been included in the exercise plan and invitations to attend have been diarised accordingly.

The meeting must be structured and the pause after the exercise conclusion provides the opportunity to examine all the information captured and using it, for instance, to stimulate discussions. In addition to those aspects of the business that the exercise focused upon, account should also be made of any broader organisational issues that may have arisen.

4.4.3 Writing the exercise report

Preparing and publishing a post exercise report is almost as important as the exercise itself. The report provides documentary evidence of what happened, what went well, what could have been done better and what went badly. Without this report, there is a very good chance that any verbally agreed action plan will never be delivered.

Ideally an exercise report should cover:

- an overview of the planning process, objectives, scope, projects plans, any relevant meeting minutes, a breakdown of the scenario, a list of attendees and the duration of their attendance if part time, etc.

- a breakdown of discussions and decisions made during the exercise and any subsequent actions (or in-actions).

- feedback, along with lessons learned including observations and recommendations relating to the exercise process.

- future action plan with defined target dates, owners and priorities.

Before its final distribution, a draft report should be distributed amongst the attendees to provide them with the chance to review it, along with the opportunity to make any further comments or flag corrections.

4.5 Validating outsourced products and services

Some organisations that outsource the creation and/or delivery of their products and services have occasionally appeared confused about where the responsibility rests for exercising of these outsourced components. Indeed, from the wider perspective, where does the responsibility rest with the entire business continuity arrangements for these products and services? While the outsourcing provider would be expected to demonstrate that the level of validation it executes is of an acceptable standard to its client, responsibility to ensure that validation is undertaken remains very firmly with the client. In fact, make no mistake, the overall responsibility for BCM remains with the client organisation and not the outsource supplier.

This is also a prime example where it would be fitting for both client and supplier to cooperate on some form of joint exercises. Furthermore, I would expect all key suppliers, not just outsourcing suppliers, to be able to demonstrate that their own BCM arrangements stand up to scrutiny, and that their own priorities complement those of your own organisation.

I, personally, always have an unhealthy suspicion of suppliers that are reluctant to share their BCM details with you. This is particularly true when, whatever reasons or excuses they offer for not sharing the information with you, you get the impression that the level of gibberish being directed at you has reached Olympic standards.

Recently, one BCM regulated client of mine was facing a similar problem, leaving them feeling potentially exposed by the lack of cooperation that was forthcoming from this particular supplier. The latter appeared to be trying to hide behind a veil of secrecy constructed around a 'need to know' basis. Ultimately, when contract renewal time came round, my client was quite blunt and gave this supplier four options:

1. Attain ISO22301 certification, or
2. Allow us to audit your BCM arrangements including your exercising results, or
3. Allow us to appoint an independent external auditor to review your BCMS at the supplier's expense, or
4. We find another supplier who meets both our business needs and BCM criterion.

Had this not ruffled a few supplier feathers and galvanised them into action, the default was option four.

Unfortunately, this had not been resolved as this book went to print. To be continued ...

4.6 Running unannounced exercises

I know that many of my business continuity professional colleagues do not necessarily favour running an unannounced exercise for a variety of reasons. Now it is true to say that I was brought up on a diet that was a blend of both announced and unannounced exercises and consequently I am comfortable using either approach. Initially, my experiences were almost entirely IT disaster recovery flavoured, although as time has passed I have been involved in unannounced exercises that have been solely business focused without any IT disaster recovery implications at all. Consequently, I consider running an exercise with no prior warning to be a valid part of the exercising tool kit.

Do we really need to remind ourselves that incidents and crises rarely oblige us by giving due notice of any impending inconvenience and disruption they are about to cause? But look, I know that there are organisations that claim that they do not approve of the concept of unannounced exercising. One client explicitly told me that it was not their policy to engage in unannounced exercises. Ok that's fair enough but I enquired whether they held building evacuation drills which he confirmed they did. "How much notice do you give staff that there will be a drill?" "Sometimes we tell them the day before sometimes we don't." "So you do hold unannounced exercises." The penny dropped.

I talked about unannounced evacuations in Chapter One. Now please make no mistake, evacuating a building is a live rehearsal which could be part of a denial of access exercise that would have the potential to be disruptive. To me this begs the question *"What's the difference between evacuating a building or exercising other parts of the BCP without warning"*? Apart from other exercises having a different scope and critical success factors, it may simply be just the level of complexity that varies.

Another key consideration regarding adopting unannounced exercising, relates to the suitability of organisations' type of business. Some would lend themselves more readily to unannounced exercises than others. I always considered the financial sector to be an area that might well be opposed to live unannounced exercising and yet I recently came across a UK Financial Services Authority paper that explicitly mentioned it as an option. But in addition to avoiding the creation of operational and reputational risks to the business, the health and safety of staff must remain of paramount importance.

Ok, now before those of you who are less experienced in BCP validation go charging off and start running unannounced exercises, please take note. If an organisation is actually new to business continuity then live exercises, let alone live unannounced exercises, should be off limits. Learn to walk before you run should be the approach. Section 1.1 talks about organisations moving from a state of unconscious incompetence to one of unconscious competence. Unless an organisation considers itself to have reached the latter, then again, unannounced live exercising is probably not a good thing.

But apart from evacuation drills, in my view unannounced exercises should only be sanctioned by organisations that have attained a high level of business continuity maturity. That is to say the overall workforce has reached that level of unconscious competence and they don't even need to think about what they have to do, they just get on with it.

I am aware of some organisations that have relocated their entire business to their designated fall-back location but without interrupting ICT. So from the external client perspective, it seemed to be seamless business as usual.

But you should always perform a thorough risk assessment and get management sign off before an unannounced exercise. Please keep in mind how an exercise might affect your clients and how to minimise, if not avoid, these risks all together. Think about what we did with the building closure case study. We prevented clients coming by pre-booking all the meeting room suites designated for client use (please see 6.5).

The biggest danger from any form of live exercise, announced or unannounced, is that if it goes wrong it could be to the detriment of your business. About two years ago, I was running the Business Continuity Institute's five-day Good Practice Guidelines course that prepares candidates to sit the BCI's certificate examination. One of the attendees was a director from an insurance broker and she made a point which is certainly worth remembering. She said that before you embark on any form of live exercise, it is worth touching base with your insurers because if things go pear shaped and the business suffers as a consequence, you could invalidate any business interruption insurance that you have. A sobering thought which made me wonder how many organisations are unwittingly jeopardising their insurance cover with every live exercise that they conduct.

I have found in some organisations that business continuity can often be put onto the back burner in favour of whatever the issue of the day happens to be. I believe that by living with the reality that an unannounced exercise could happen at any time, it keeps participants more focused, especially if their business continuity responsibilities are incentivised by measurable objectives (see *Chapter 10* – Performance appraisal).

Finally, one of the questions I was asked in a validation webinar that I ran for the BCI, was about running exercises without warning. In effect, the attendee wanted to know if I had ever run an unannounced exercise that involved the senior management team. I had to admit that I had not. Unless you have a very generous and unusually flexible mandate for your exercise programme, you will invariably have to go to senior management for sign off of what you are proposing to do. Consequently, it would be difficult, if not impossible, to surprise senior management in this way.

4.7 Assessing the costs and risks

Let us be up front about this – whatever form of exercising technique you choose to undertake, there is always a cost involved and invariably an associated risk. When presenting a validation programme proposal to management, someone is bound to ask *"How much is this going to cost?"* or *"How much time do you expect my team to have to spend on this?"*. The reality is, of course, that whatever you do, there will always be a cost involved, even if it is only the time it takes two or three people to perform a desk check or a walkthrough exercise. The more people you need to involve and the more time you need to take, along with any other resources (e.g. room, equipment hire, etc.) you may need, the more expensive it will become. Moreover, if your organisation is inexperienced in validation matters, you may opt to use a business continuity specialist to help you negotiate the learning curve (please refer to Section 11 – Using consultants to help you).

Then we have to consider the inherent risks involved. There may well be risks involved by taking employees away from their day jobs, especially if junior and less experienced employees are used to replace them in what might be a critical role. However, there will invariably be an even greater risk when you are performing a live exercise. It is worth taking a look at the live, unannounced exercise in the case study in Section 6.5 – *Sorry, you cannot evacuate the building before lunch* is *finished*. A thorough risk assessment was undertaken in an effort to mitigate the chances of the exercise creating a catastrophe if it all went pear shaped.

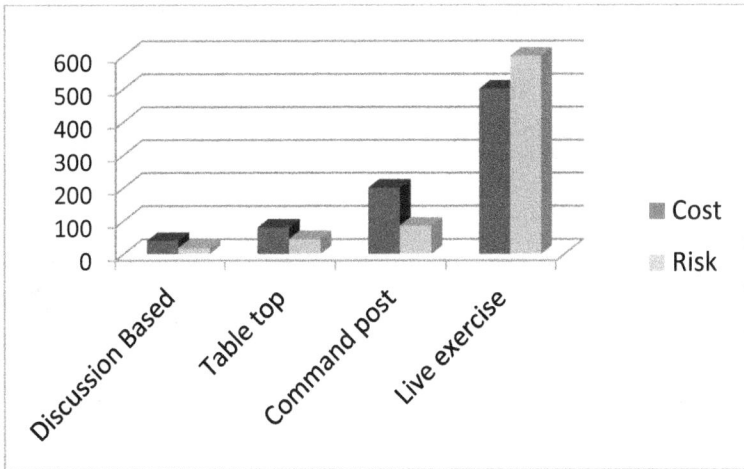

Figure 16: Cost and risk implications by exercise type

From 'discussion based' exercises on the left through to 'live exercises' on the right, the chart in *Figure 16* gives an indication of how both the costs and associated risks will inevitably rise. Despite having been involved in many live tests and exercises over the years, there was something brought to my attention around two years ago which I had never even considered which has a direct influence on the cost base. I was running a BCI licensed training course which was preparing the students to sit the BCI certificate examination (CBCI). While discussing live exercising, one of the students who was the business development director for an insurance broker, pointed out that if the exercise went wrong and you actually caused an incident, it could invalidate your insurance cover. Ouch! She likened it to starting your car in the street, walking away and leaving it unattended. If it was then stolen in your absence, it is unlikely that the event will have impressed your insurer, who may well reject any claim you subsequently make. It was here the pupil turned teacher strongly advised that you discussed your live exercising plans with your insurers. They may feel an extra premium is called for to underwrite any additional risk that you could be generating through the exercise.

One other major consideration which will have a direct impact on your exercising budget is what type of exercises you run and how frequently. For example, you would expect an organisation to undertake far more 'discussion based' exercises than 'live' exercises. The former may only involve two or three people and would have a low level of complexity, while the live exercise could invariably be very expensive and have a high degree of complexity. It would demand the involvement of considerably more of your employees including senior management. Moreover, depending upon the nature of the exercise, it may also require the support of your suppliers. So, in addition to possibly having a direct effect on your business as usual activity along with the potential loss of revenue, suppliers may also require some form of compensation too.

Do keep in mind that if exercising occurs outside of normal business hours, while your productivity may remain uninterrupted, depending on the contractual agreements in place with your workforce, overtime payments may have to be budgeted. This may apply to your suppliers too, so make sure you are familiar with their out of hours callout and overtime rates.

One organisation I provided some consultancy for decided that they wanted to establish how quickly their internet service provider (ISP) could run a network cable into their warm disaster recovery site (DRS) and would it match their recovery time objectives (RTO). Even though the ISP said they could meet the RTO requirement, the organisation included this within the budget paid to the supplier to demonstrate that they could. As the organisation did not want to pay the cost of having the cable permanently attached to their DRS, on completion of the exercise, they requested its removal.

Figure 17 on page 92, demonstrates the relationship between the frequency and complexity of the various exercising categories. This illustration was used in the 2005 edition of the GPG and although the exercising category names have since changed, it effectively emphasises the relationships between the categories, frequency and complexity.

Type	Process	Participants	Fre-quency	Comp-lexity
Desk check	Review and challenge plan contents	• Author of plan • Independent checker	HIGH	LOW
Walk-through plan	Extend desk checks to check interaction and the roles of the participants	• Author of plan • Main participants		
Simulation	Incorporates associated plans: • Business • Site/buildings • Communications • Public relations • ITDR • BCM resource recovery suppliers	• Main participants • Facilitator • Observers • Co-ordinators • Umpires		
Functions	Moves to and recreates one, or a number of, business functions at an alternative pre-planned site	• Employees and staff in specific business area • Facilitator • Observers • Co-ordinators • BC resource recovery suppliers		
Full plan	Close down of entire site/building and relocation of work	• Staff required for recovery activities included in BC plans • Facilitator • Observers • Co-ordinators • Umpire • BC resource recovery suppliers	LOW	HIGH

Figure 17: Exercising types and methods
Source: (Elliot, et al., 1999, p. 84)

CHAPTER 5: SELECTED SCENARIOS

"I have not failed. I've just found 10,000 ways that won't work." – Thomas Edison

While there are several scenario candidate topics I could have chosen to write about in this chapter, I have selected three pet subjects of mine – media communications, ICT disaster recovery and terrorism. Strange bed fellow you may think but most business continuity plans will have to take account of at least two of them and with the number of high-profile global terrorist attacks being reported, I'll wager that terrorism features in more BCPs than it did say a decade ago. While I have endeavoured to provide some background into each and their importance to business continuity planners, this work is essentially about how to approach exercising the plans.

5.1 Media communications

"Lack of, or poor, communication is one of the most common causes of project failure. Remember, if you don't communicate, someone else will." Mel Gosling

In the 21st century, the dissemination of news across the globe has become virtually instantaneous. Following a high-profile incident, particularly if it involves injuries or fatalities, the demand and expectation for an instant information flow can be almost insatiable. Failure by organisations to quickly deliver accurate and honest information can sometimes seem to turn communications into more of a problem than the original incident itself.

In her 2012 'Communications in a Crisis' presentation, ABTA Senior Public Relations Officer, Gillian Edwards, provides some good advice on 'Dos' and 'Don'ts' in the following table:

Do:	Don't:
Consider how to comment: statements, interviews, social media, pictures, etc. to best manage the issue	Comment without checking your facts
Act immediately to escalate the issue with colleagues	Miss deadlines
Establish and control the facts	Tell half the story/obfuscate
Check with third-parties (e.g. ABTA)	Let social media comment control the story
Get back to them on time, even with a holding statement	Use language that is over-technical, legal jargon or patronising
Find out deadlines and establish what the journalist knows	Run away!
Show your 'human' side	

Applying the above needs experience and maturity and so should be included within an organisation's validation programme.

5.1.1 Facing the press

> "*Ignoring the media when dealing with issues and crises will always prove to be a catastrophic error of judgement.*" (Regester & Larkin, 2008, p. 182)

Some of the case studies in *Chapter 6* include examples of communicating specifically via social media – more about that later. But we must not forget that the press, television and radio are still extremely powerful communication channels. While certainly not unimportant, for many of us, preparing the wording of a Tweet or Facebook posting is going to be far less daunting than standing up in front of the traditional media and making a statement or responding to questions, particularly if you find yourself looking down the lens of a TV camera.

Napoleon Bonaparte is attributed with stating that four hostile newspapers were to be more feared than a thousand bayonets. Now more than two centuries later, the media is far more complex and efficient, resulting in the dissemination of news around the globe that can be measured in nanoseconds.

Two fairly recent instances of public relations disasters come to mind which have both found themselves a place in folklore as examples of how not to behave on camera. The first was BP's former CEO, Tony Heyward, speaking about the 2010 Deepwater Horizon oil rig disaster in the Gulf of Mexico. 11 people had died and Heyward was vilified after saying on camera that "he wanted his life back". The second was Freedom Industries' President, Gary Southern, who reluctantly stood in front of a camera in 2014 and tried to explain how his company had managed to dump toxins into the River Elk that 300,000 depended upon for their potable water supply. He twice tried to avoid difficult questions by attempting to wrap up the session and walk away but at least one extremely tenacious reporter refused to let him go. To add insult to injury, he was taking sips of water from a bottle while many of the viewers watching the interview had been deprived of their drinking water supply.

Both Heyward and Southern's blunders have since been saved for posterity on YouTube.

So who should be the one responsible for standing up in front of the press, or facing a TV camera? Some CEOs take the view that it is their responsibility to do this but they may not necessarily be the person best qualified. Hopefully, the experiences of Messrs Heyward and Southern will make the point that this is not necessarily so. There are of course exceptions. Sir Richard Branson and Sir Michael Bishop's respective handling of the 2007 Virgin train crash and the 1989 BMI aircraft crash have been hailed as classic examples of excellent media public relations. Moreover, through their words, they both also showed a human caring side, something that both Heyward and Southern apparently lacked. In fact, Branson was visibly upset and he appeared close to tears when he told reporters *"It is a very sad day because of the loss of one life and the injuries caused to others"*.

In managing their communications, larger organisations often appoint media communications and public relations professionals. There are also specialist companies that offer a full range of crisis management public relations services. However, these options are likely to be a luxury that is well beyond the budgets of your average SME.

There are, of course, a plethora of public relations and communication training courses to choose from. But the spokesperson for a SME is likely to have other, non-PR related responsibilities and may get few opportunities to practise and hone their communications skills in the work environment. In addition to participating in as many relevant BCP exercises as is possible and practical, I would suggest that they:

- Watch as many television journalists as possible who are interviewing company representatives after a crisis. You will find that YouTube is a good source of material. Observe their respective technique and also the response and behaviour of the interviewees. This can provide you with some very useful material of what to do and what not to do, that can help you negotiate your own PR communication learning curve.

- Consider joining a group, such as Toastmasters International, branches of which can be found globally. This will not only give you a confidence building chance to practise speaking in public but also to think on your feet when given very limited time to gather your thoughts – not a million miles away from dealing with journalists.

5.1.2 Social media

When a crisis strikes, the speed at which social media can be exploited to 'spread the news' can be breath taking, as this example below demonstrates.

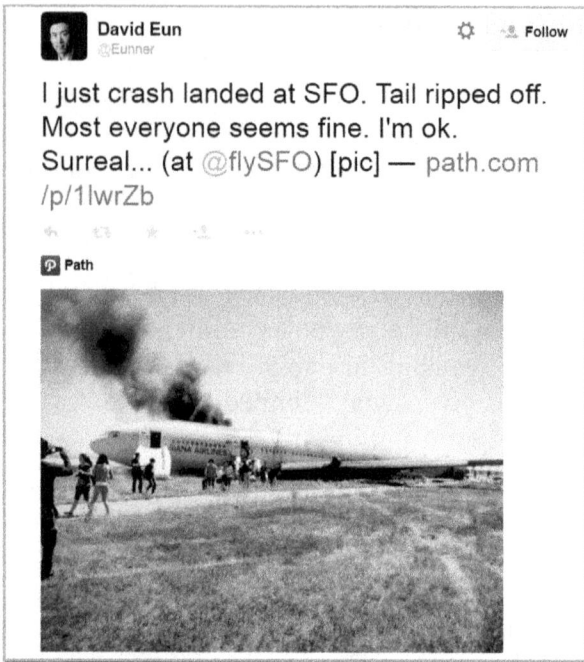

Figure 18: Tweet by air crash survivor

In the case of Asiana Flight OZ 214 crashing at San Francisco International Airport, 6 July 2013, the first report and photograph appeared on Twitter a full two minutes before the emergency evacuation slides had been deployed by cabin crew. A subsequent tweet by surviving passenger David Eun (see *Figure 18*) was retweeted over 32,000 times and was quickly picked up by several major television news networks, such as the BBC, CNN, Sky and NBC.

Aircraft manufacturer Boeing, the local fire department and National Transportation Safety Board had all issued statements on social media shortly after the crash. Such was the intensity of related information searches[3], the airline, Asiana, was almost instantly put on the back foot. However, it was still four hours after the incident before it broke its silence and posted a comment on Facebook and it was a further five hours later when it issued a press statement.

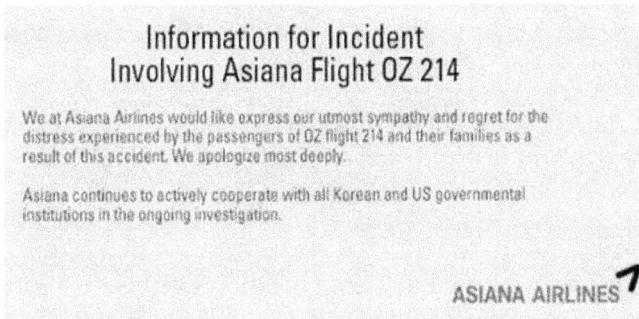

Information for Incident Involving Asiana Flight OZ 214

We at Asiana Airlines would like express our utmost sympathy and regret for the distress experienced by the passengers of OZ flight 214 and their families as a result of this accident. We apologize most deeply.

Asiana continues to actively cooperate with all Korean and US governmental institutions in the ongoing investigation.

ASIANA AIRLINES

Figure 19: Asiana Airlines Facebook post

"Tell it all, tell it fast and tell the truth." (Hicks, 2006)

With three fatalities and 49 serious injuries, what can be learned from this catastrophic situation? First and foremost, in this age of virtually instant news reporting, the speed of communication is essential. There is a growing expectation that your organisation will respond instantaneously with all the facts and report them honestly. Failure to do so may be interpreted, although potentially unjustly, in a number of negative ways, such as you are unprepared, not in control of the situation, or that you have adopted an overly casual and indifferent attitude. It must be remembered that many of your

---

3 A similar experience happened at Glasgow Airport after the 2007 attempted bombing. The traffic to the airport website alone rose from an average of 6,000 hits per week to 130,000 during the week immediately following the incident.

stakeholders will be demanding answers or reassurance. Any delays in information dissemination may be interpreted as a reluctance or an inability to act decisively. This in turn could be seen as being symptomatic of a questionable ability, in this case of operating an airline. Moreover, you will need to be actively following the popular social media websites, such as Twitter and Facebook to monitor what disparaging remarks are being made about your organisation, especially by accounts that have large followings.

> *"Fail to communicate effectively and you risk losing the trust and confidence of your customers, or worse: your company's reputation takes a nose dive."* (Finegan, 2013)

Running a social media communication exercise is probably within the capability of many organisations – providing they steer clear of live exercising. Unless the organisation is really on top of its game vis-à-vis social media communications, I would strongly recommend that they consider using the services of one of the many companies that offer social media simulation in a crisis management situation. Although it is not my intent to endorse any of their respective products through the pages of this book, there are a number of reputable options listed on the Internet.

5.2 ICT disaster recovery

> *"Disaster recovery testing has been around for more than 30 years but, unfortunately, most companies are exercising their disaster recovery and business continuity plans and capabilities like it was still the 1970s. No evolution. No improvement. No relevance to actual disaster scenarios."* (Beattie, 2014)

Since IT disaster recovery is the generally accepted modern day origin of business continuity, it may seem somewhat inequitable that it has been confined to just a section in this book. However, as business continuity professionals will appreciate, disaster recovery is now quite rightly considered just part of the BCM story, albeit an important part, rather than the whole story as it used to be.

Back in the day, you protected your data by backing up to tape, stored at least one copy in a safe and secure remote location, and then used that data to test your disaster recovery capability or, indeed, used it to recover from a live incident. Without a useable set of back-up data, your business could be placed in very serious jeopardy if you lost it.

5.2.1 Data recovery testing

If someone wants to take a photograph, they basically need three things − a camera, a subject and light. Depending on your needs, you can select any one of a massive assortment of cameras, from the very cheap and cheerful, right up to the top of the range professional cameras, while the choice of subjects is just about endless. However, without light (whether ambient or artificial) you will simply not be able to take your photograph. This is not dissimilar to IT disaster recovery set-ups. You can have the Rolls Royce of disaster recovery fall-back environment ready to motor but without any data to recover, you are going absolutely nowhere, except to say your business could be heading for extinction.

Many organisations, particularly large companies, do regularly back up their data, although I do wonder how many actually test whether they can recover from that back up. One client used tape as its preferred back up medium but it was discovered in a DR test that the tape drive used to create the back ups, and the tape drive installed at the recovery site, were incompatible. Best to discover that sort of thing before you need to recover for real.

But even now, 40 years after I experienced my first disaster recovery trial, I continue to be amazed by those companies that still do not back up their data or, almost as bad, keep their backups in close proximity to their primary data source. Such an example came to light in 2007. Following an explosion and subsequent fire at Aztec Chemicals in Crewe, UK, their woefully inadequate data backup procedure left the management believing that both their primary and backup data had been lost in a building gutted by fire. Three days after the explosion, on discovering that their backup tape had remarkably survived, an enormously relieved Financial Director, Carl Chadwick, remarked:

> *"We were unbelievably lucky – unbelievably lucky! Without that tape I just don't know how we would have recovered."* (Clark, 2014, p. 111)

Having since had the opportunity to reflect, Chadwick had come to the conclusion that Aztec's backup procedure had been '*sheer stupidity*'. But now with us well into the 21st century, in addition to the tried and tested magnetic tape method, there are other perfectly good backup solutions that can be adopted. Moreover, as each decade passes, backing up your data continues to get easier, whether your organisation is a large multinational corporation or a SME.

> *"It's a fact of modern life that archiving data is essential to prevent a data disaster. Still, something like one third of computers are never backed up, according to 2,257 respondents in a recent poll."*
> (Nadel, 2012)

I understand that this rather alarming statistic relates primarily to SMEs. Here, Nadel suggests that the need to back up data is synonymous with modern day life. I would argue that it was ever thus and this '*need*' certainly predates the digital age. All computers have done in that respect is to make it much easier for us to archive and retrieve our data – some cynics might say "*lose it too*".

It is worth remembering that regardless of the size of your organisation, you are not restricted to using just one of the following examples. In fact, I would urge you, if you don't already, to use more than one medium to back up that all important data of yours. Your options include:

- CDs
- DVDs
- External hard drives
- Pen drives (although I feel they are not as resilient as other medium and are more easily 'misplaced')
- Storage Area Network (SAN) replication
- Clustering
- Mirroring
- The Cloud – remember that the Cloud is not some magical or mystical panacea, and by using it means you have outsourced the storage of your data to a third party supplier. Like any other supplier, these suppliers can fail and indeed some have, such as Nirvanix and Symantec's Backup Exec.cloud Service in 2013. I would recommend that anyone using Cloud based services should look at alternative means of back up to avoid creating, and falling foul of, a single point of failure, even if it means using another Cloud service supplier.

"When it comes to advice about backing up data, conventional wisdom today insists you should use a Cloud solution. That's a smart move, but the same is true in reverse as well. If you store everything in the Cloud, you might not be able to access your data when outages and other failures occur." (Grady, 2014)

How you back up your data, with what frequency and how quickly you will need to recover it, are criterion that you should have considered as part of defining your business continuity strategies, and then developed as part of your BCP and ICT disaster recovery plans. Consequently, I do not intend to say anymore explaining how to back up and restore your data because as we say in the UK that should be tantamount to *"teaching my grandmother to suck eggs"*. Suffice it to say that you can use the full range of techniques covered in Section 4.2.1 to perform both tests and exercises on data retrieval and recovery. Should you go down the sensible route and choose to use multiple backup options, please ensure that you can recover from all of them and not just rely on only one source of data.

I would like to make one final point which is by way of a warning about managing your data backups. If you store large numbers of magnetic tapes as part of your off-site vital record arrangements, make sure that you can always quickly locate the tapes you need for a recovery, for which you will need a disciplined process for storing them. This is especially true if you are working to very short recovery time objectives. Moreover, it is worth considering incorporating an exercise in the validation programme that periodically restores the data to check its currency and validity.

5.2.2 Exercising for your ICT environment

For me, back in the 1970s, planning and exercising a disaster recovery trial was a great deal easier than it is today. I started out working in a mainframe environment with only batch processing – that is punched cards in and printed paper out. Yes, I know, how quaint and primitive! But in its day it was most definitely state of the art technology. Even an online service was still several years away. We had no Internet to worry about and no desktop environment or mobile devices to accommodate. Most of the exercises we ran were parallel tests with no risk to the production environment.

How things have changed. These days there are many more permutations and combinations of ways to approach disaster recovery before you even contemplate the technical advances that have been made in the past 40 years. How you approach it will be very much dependent upon what you need for a recovery. If you are a one-man-band with a single laptop, perhaps with an Internet connection, then your disaster recovery approach should be relatively simplistic. However, if your organisation has a designated recovery location, whether you have opted for a hot, warm or cold standby site will also have a significant bearing on your recovery plans. Hot is the most expensive option and provides a high availability service by replicating your production environment. It also implies that the organisation has very short recovery time objectives. At the other extreme, a cold site could just be an empty building, perhaps with nothing more than power and HVAC facilities which implies you have the luxury of time to recover your operation.

Alternatively, you may have outsourced your recovery, or indeed your entire operation, to a reputable supplier, such as SunGard or IBM. Don't forget to factor in smartphones and tablets, not of course forgetting any Cloud based dependencies that you may have. The following diagram has been reproduced with the kind permission of Helen Porter, marketing director at the DSM Group. It provides some indication of the type of threats that should be considered when preparing an exercise, and that is without mentioning what is becoming every CIO's nightmare – the ever growing cyber threat. It also nicely emphasises the point that modern day IT DR planners have to deal with something of a moving target, as technology marches on relentlessly.

Figure 20: Evolving technology adds to the DR challenges
Source: (DSM Group, 2015)

Those organisations that justify setting up a server room for their primary ICT environment, will have a couple of options to consider in terms of where they will locate the server room – either in house or outsourced. The same applies for their disaster recovery fall-back arrangements – that is 'in house' or outsourced. I should stress that by using an 'in house' disaster recovery site, I am certainly not advocating that primary and DR server rooms are located in the same building, or even in close proximity, but are merely under the organisation's control. However, there are some large organisations that also have what I refer to as a requirement for a 'secondary DR fall-back' service.

This 'belt and bracers' disaster recovery approach may seem something of an overkill but in every instance that I have come across, it has been done with good reason and with a rock solid business case behind it.

In the following diagram I have suggested four possible configurations for organisations that opt for a secondary DR facility. I personally have come across Configuration's One, Two and Three. Although Configuration Four has so far eluded me, I can see no reason why it should not exist somewhere on the planet. I am yet to come across a justification for a configuration that has 'outsourced' as the primary service and 'in house' as the DR fall-back service.

Configuration example	Primary ICT service	DR fall-back facility	Secondary DR fall-back facility
One	In house	In house	In house
Two	In house	In house	Outsourced
Three	In house	Outsourced	Outsourced
Four	Outsourced	Outsourced	Outsourced

Figure 21: Primary and disaster recovery location option examples

For outsourced, you can also substitute 'Cloud' because by using the Cloud all you are doing is outsourcing your data processing.

5.2.2.1 Getting started

Ok, let's get to the heart of the matter, what exactly should you be exercising and how should you be exercising it? Essentially, the types of exercise described in Section 4.2.1 work for disaster recovery exercising too. However, there are a few important differences which I will cover below. But first, keep in mind that although it is not essential, ICT disaster recovery exercising can generally be undertaken independently of other BCP exercising:

- The 'big picture' that you are ultimately working towards means that you can demonstrate that you can recover your environment within the recovery time objectives including for multiple failures[4] that could be the result of a variety of threats.

- Testing: initially you are likely to be engaged in more testing which means you are looking for a 'pass' or 'fail' outcome. Start out by working with an individual component (e.g. rebuild a server, etc.) and then expand the scope to combine a series of related components.

5.2.2.2 Parallel testing

A parallel testing exercise would normally use the ICT disaster recovery environment, and should not in any way touch the primary systems or networks which continue with

---

[4] I was once requested by a business continuity manager I was working with to accompany him to a meeting with the ICT department. The head of ICT confidently informed us that exercises had proved that every RTO could be met. I asked if they could meet all the RTOs if a multiple failure was experienced. At this point, I was told that I was not welcome at the meeting and was asked to leave for asking awkward questions. It later emerged that the answer to my question was 'No'.

the business as usual activity. This approach enables hands-on validation of DR plans in a pseudo live environment but without the risk of any disruption to the business operation. This can include:

- Acquiring replacement equipment. In some DR plans, you use systems that the organisation already owns as recovery systems. In others, the organisation must purchase recovery systems. For the purposes of parallel testing, you may need to alter the plans somewhat, so those purchases don't actually happen. A viable alternative would be to lease the systems that you need for the duration of the parallel test.

- Side-by-side transactions. Depending on the nature of the business process and IT systems you're parallel testing, you may be able to run some, or all, of the actual business transactions through both the actual systems and the parallel test systems. The DR project team needs to decide what criteria to use when determining which transactions to run on the DR systems.

- Actual load or simulated load. The nature of the business might require that you perform only a small portion of transactions to validate the test. But for the test to be valid, the recovery system may need to take a full workload, even if you run only dummy data through it. Testing may also require both types of tests (small numbers of real transactions, plus a full workload test) to validate the correct operation of the systems.

- External interfaces. Make the parallel test as much like the real production system it's mimicking as you can. But you need to simulate some parts of the test so you can avoid certain undesirable events. For example, if an application sends transactions to a bank or payment processor for payment, you might want to avoid having the test system also transmit those transactions, or else your organisation incurs twice the number and amount of payments. You may also need to apply this principle to other internal applications.

- Make the test as real as possible. Despite all of the limitations I mention in this list, the point of the parallel test is to determine if your DR plan will work during a disaster. Consequently, leave the DR test personnel alone to figure out the hard stuff. The procedures won't be perfect, and you should constrain the test personnel somewhat – and somehow – so they can't cheat by overcoming obstacles more easily than they would be able to during an actual disaster.

Even with seemingly adequate precautions, things can go wrong with parallel testing, which can interfere with ongoing business processes. But you can get considerable benefits from parallel testing: Real-world experience in building and starting recovery systems and running them through their paces to see if they can support critical processes in a real disaster. Although parallel testing is considerably more valuable than walkthrough testing for validating plans, parallel testing falls short of actually supporting critical business processes. Another activity, however, can erase all doubt as to whether recovery systems can do the job – cutover testing. I discuss cutover testing in Section 5.2.2.3.

5.2.2.3 Cutover testing

"Cutover testing is deadly serious business. It is without doubt, the DR test with the highest amount of risk. A cutover test is a kind of heart-lung bypass

during open heart surgery – the consequences of failure are tremendous." (Gregory, 2008, p. 230)

Cutover tests are not dissimilar to parallel tests, although with a very significant difference. Parallel testing stops short of processing live data. However, unless you are using clustering or replication, in an ICT sense, cutover testing is when you might start sweating in earnest because if something goes wrong it will be the live environment that is directly affected.

I hope I am preaching to the converted when I say that this will take a lot of preparation and planning. From my own experience, I know that creating a detailed critical path plan certainly helps, as it identifies the interdependent tasks that will need to be undertaken.

Your plan will be designed to transfer processing to your disaster recovery site when your primary location has been compromised in some way. However, you do have a few other considerations to take account of when conducting a test. First, ensure that your DR environment is operational and the critical applications are running. At this point, the primary site is still operational and should remain so until you have established that the DR site is ready to become the live environment. This reduces the down time that will be experienced by your organisation and its clientele, regardless of how generous or not the recovery time objective is for a real recovery. When you have reached the 'ready to transfer' point in the operation, take the live system offline and commence the transfer of transaction data to the DR site. How you do this will be dependent upon your configuration, although you will need to ensure data integrity is maintained at all times. Once complete, enable the DR site so it becomes the primary site.

Having proved their cutover plan works, most organisations would look to revert to the primary system, for which a plan will be required detailing how to restore the primary site. That said, there are some larger organisations that regularly switch from primary site to disaster fall-back site and back to primary, such that it really does not matter which site they are operating from. Of course to do this, both environments need to be compatible, so no degradation of service is experienced when processing from either site. This was, in fact, something I got used to over 30 years ago. The level of confidence amongst both management and ICT staff when a switch was made, was very high because the whole activity was well-rehearsed and worked like a well-oiled machine. Ok, so having produced your cutover plan, you do not start by trying it out in a live environment. Like any other plan, first subject it to the other exercise types described in Section 4.2.1.

5.2.2.4 Managing replication and clustering facilities

Exactly how you configure your clustering and replication technologies will determine how easy (or not) it will be to activate a cutover from production to disaster recovery environments. Essentially, with this technology it is possible for your production environment to be simultaneously running in the DR site too. So the emphasis must be on exploiting the technology to provide the benefit of instant switching between sites.

5.3 Terrorism

> *"Many organisations have made themselves feel really good about their crisis management preparedness by*

validating their arrangements with scenarios that are frankly far too tame." (Sterling, et al., 2012, p. 163)

While terrorism has become a global scourge, there are some countries that take it more seriously than others. For example, the UK and US are no strangers to both internal and transnational terrorist attacks. Statistics collected by Maryland University's START programme, run in conjunction with Homeland Security, show that in 2012 there were 5,685 global terrorist attacks and 19,355 associated fatalities. The following year that had substantially risen to 7,967 and 28,488 respectively.

These attacks can use any one of a number of modus operandi, such as bombings, shootings, CBRN and cyber attacks, or any combination. Person Borne Improvised Explosive Devices (PBIED), often referred to as a suicide bomber, and Vehicle Borne Improvised Explosives Devices (VBIED), have become a popular and effective means of terrorist attack. In some parts of the world Animal Borne Improvised Explosive Devices (ABIED) are still used, where terrorists may opt to use a donkey or horse to facilitate the attack.

However, while organisations can incorporate terrorism as part of their BCM arrangements, it would be very difficult and potentially very expensive to independently create a realistic live exercise that simulates a terrorist attack. This is equally true whether the organisation is the target, or runs the risk of suffering from collateral damage. One London hotel security manager I met pointed out that the hotel building was located very close to several prime terrorist targets and that collateral damage was considered to be a very serious threat.

In 2004, the Metropolitan Police created 'Project Griffin', in an initiative designed to protect the country's cities and communities from the terrorist threat.

"Project Griffin was developed by the City of London Police and formally introduced in London in April 2004 as a joint venture between the City and Metropolitan police forces. Its remit was to advise and familiarise managers, security officers and employees of large public and private sector organisations across the capital on security, counter-terrorism and crime prevention issues." (Project Griffin, 2014)

Griffin has since become a nationwide initiative and is now supported by Project Argus which is a National Counter Terrorism Security Office (NaCTSO) led initiative. The 'Argus Team' works with businesses and other organisations to evaluate their state of readiness for a terrorist attack.

"It achieves this by guiding people through a simulated multimedia attack which identifies the measures that can assist in preventing, handling and recovering from such an incident. It explores what is likely to happen in the event of a terrorist attack. It highlights the importance of being prepared and having the necessary plans in place to help safeguard staff, visitors and assets." (Heart of London, 2015)

Argus events are interactive and audience participation is essential in maximising the benefit for the attendees. UK police forces also run exercises that focus on the CBRN threat. *Chapter 6* includes case studies of 'bomb scares' and 'active shooter' rehearsals, along with an exercise run by the FBI that simulated a CBRN attack. For more information about what exercises and training is available in your country of operation, may I suggest that you contact your local police or security services.

5.4 Scenario summary

While this chapter has only looked at three scenarios, there are, of course, others that organisations should plan for and validate, such as denial of access (DoA) and lack of staff. Deciding which to plan for should be driven by the output from your 'business impact analysis' and 'risk assessment' activities that you will have undertaken at the beginning of the BCM lifecycle. However, for your convenience, *Chapter 6* includes a number of validation case studies that includes examples of both DoA (see 6.1 and 6.5) and lack of staff (see 6.4 and 6.8).

CHAPTER 6: LIVE REHEARSAL CASE STUDIES

"In a crisis you will not rise to your (stakeholders) expectations, but fall to your level of preparedness – how prepared are you?" – Wayne Harrop

This chapter contains a series of case studies of live exercises, some of which I was personally involved with, while others are situations that I was aware of. In the main, the exercises went largely to plan and achieved their respective objectives. Even so, each will provide the reader with lessons to be learned and things to be avoided.

Where at all possible and practical, adding a sense of realism can only benefit the participants. For example, inviting the local fire services to support a fire evacuation drill can add credibility to the proceedings, especially if the exercise is unannounced. Volunteers can be made up to appear injured and mobile triage units and pop-up hospitals can be drafted in to deal with 'casualties'.

One of the modern day phenomena being witnessed in both BCP validation and dealing with genuine incidents, is the increasing use of social media. This can work both for and against organisations, especially when an incident is visible to the public and they are posting reports on the likes of Facebook and Twitter in real time. The earlier example of the uploading of photographs of the Asiana aircraft crash at San Francisco International Airport only moments after the crash illustrates the point. The first photograph had been posted on twitter even before the aircraft's emergency exit slides had been deployed and several hours before the airline had been able to make a statement.

6.1 From a full dress rehearsal to the real thing inside four months

Scenario

Driven by the Hong Kong Monetary Authority (HKMA), this 'denial of access' (DoA) exercise was held in Hong Kong and involved 55 financial organisations based in the territory. Any one of a number of threats can result in a DoA situation which may be nothing more than a minor short-term inconvenience. However, a DoA can last for several weeks, or even months, and organisations need to be prepared to react accordingly or suffer the consequences. In one extreme case, following the 1996 IRA terrorist bombing of Manchester in the UK, emergency services created an exclusion zone which remained in situ for several months, forcing over 200 ill-prepared businesses into bankruptcy.

> *"The drill assumed that due to unexpected events, the headquarters or other important operating sites of banks in Central as well as the HKMA's office became inaccessible. Hence, banks and the HKMA need to simulate the activation of their BCPs and operate in their respective back-up offices. The exercise sought to test the reliability and stability of the communications between the HKMA's and participating banks' back-up offices. At the same time, banks were required to submit situation reports to the HKMA's back-up office."* (Chan, 2014)

Simulated duration: Several weeks

Detail

During October 2014 I was in Hong Kong. On my return to the UK I was asked if I had seen the riots. While there had been some isolated violent clashes reported by the media, what I personally witnessed was a series of peaceful pro-democracy protests by tens of thousands of local inhabitants. They were seeking what many of us in the western world take for granted – universal suffrage.

Known as 'Occupy Central' or the 'Umbrella Revolution', four sites across the territory, three on Hong Kong Island and one in Kowloon, were seized by the protestors. Major thoroughfares were barricaded and permanent campsites were set up on what would normally have been busy arterial roads. Barricades remained in place for two months before police started to make a concerted effort to remove them.

Approximately three months earlier, the Hong Kong Monetary Authority (HKMA) had conducted a business continuity exercise involving 55 local banks. The scenario was 'denial of access' and the HKMA was looking to validate the reliability and stability of the communications between HKMA and the backup sites for the participating banks.

"Central is the hub of banking and financial operations in Hong Kong, and we do not want to see disruptions of the normal operation of banks. As the supervisory authority for banks in Hong Kong, the HKMA must ensure that banks have in place robust business continuity plans so that the core functions of the banking system can be maintained even in extreme circumstances, such as inaccessibility of offices in Central.

Overall speaking, the drill was conducted smoothly and the activation of back-up offices and the various communication channels including email, telephone and fax functioned properly. We are satisfied with the outcome of the drill." Norman Chan (Chan, 2014)

This exercise was well timed, as several banks including HSBC Holdings, Hang Seng Bank, Citibank and Australia and New Zealand Banking Group were directly affected by the Occupy Central protests which kicked-off at the end of September. As journalist Tiffany Ap reported:

> *"At its peak on 29 September, the number of closures totalled 36 branches, offices and ATMs of 20 banks."* (Ap, 2014)

6.2 Guildhall filled with smoke for training exercise

Scenario

The second floor of the Portsmouth Guildhall in the UK is unoccupied and provided the setting for local firefighters to rehearse their fire and rescue procedures within an office building. The designated area was filled with smoke and six dummies had to be located and rescued by the emergency services.

Simulated duration: Hours

Detail

In the UK, 23 October 2013 witnessed the Portsmouth Guildhall being used to make a realistic scenario as part of a training exercise for the local Fire and Rescue Service (FRS). The 'incident' was attended by 20 firefighters and three fire engines plus two smaller FRS vehicles.

The second floor was filled with smoke and the firefighters had the task of locating and rescuing six dummies that were acting as casualties. An exclusion zone was set up as part of the exercise and a section of the Guildhall Square was cordoned off. Bruce Gordon, manager at Portsmouth's Cosham fire station, said:

> *"Every year each group has to run a certain amount of training exercises. This is about training and testing the procedures and knowing the risks. Today the Guildhall being the size it is, is one major risk. We have some dummies on the second floor – which is disused – and filled with smoke. The firefighters know there are 'persons reported as missing and will have to make decisions as to what to do."* (Mistry, 2013)

While remaining in the City of Portsmouth, at this point I would like to take you off at a slight tangent. For a time, I worked in sight of Whale Island in Portsmouth Harbour, where the Royal Navy has a specialist state-of-the-art firefighting school. From my desk, I would often see a plume of black smoke erupt from the island. The threat of a fire at sea is taken very seriously and every sailor must complete a course at the Navy's specialist training centre. Unlike the earlier Guildhall example search and rescue, the fires they face are real.

> *"Nothing is more dangerous on board a ship or submarine than fire – confined spaces, toxic substances, intense heat, claustrophobia, ammunition 'cooking off'. It (the training school) replicates compartments on board a warship, such as engine rooms, machinery control rooms, mess decks, galleys and passageways. The fires inside are gas-powered – making them environmentally-friendly – and supported by smoke generators, can be controlled by tutors."* (Royal Navy, 2015)

Now you may argue that this is basic on-the-job training. However, I beg to differ. While all Royal Navy ships have specialist firefighting teams, it also ensures that ever sailor has reached that 'Unconscious Competence' level discussed in Section 1.1.

Like the Royal Navy, the merchant marine also takes the fire threat seriously. Several training schools exist in the UK that are approved by the Government's Maritime and Coastguard Agency (MCA).

> *"Fire remains one of the top three causes of loss for marine vessels in the World Fleet."* (Royal Institution of Naval Architects, 2014)

There are many examples of both qualitative and quantitative maritime fire risk assessments in the public domain. To ignore the threat of maritime fire would be tantamount to gross negligence, regardless of whether by naval or commercial shipping. Again, it is a case of practice makes perfect.

6.3 Airport simulates runway aircraft collision

Scenario

A light aircraft and an airliner with 50 passengers on board collided on the runway and the airliner caught fire. Emergency services had to extinguish the blaze and rescue the passengers, many of whom were reported to have injuries sustained during the incident.

Simulated duration: Hours

Detail

In line with International Civil Aviation Organisation regulations, 12 November 2013 saw a fierce blaze erupt, as an exercise commenced aimed at validating both Malta

International Airport's response capability, plus the country's emergency response.

Supported by Emirates Airlines, around 200 people took part in the test including the Civil Protection Department, Armed Forces Malta, plus fire and ambulance crews. Medical teams from Malta's principal hospital, Mater Dei Hospital (MDH), set up a field hospital to treat casualties. While firemen doused the flames with foam, face mask wearing stretcher bearers began locating and removing the 'injured' passengers from a smoke filled aircraft.

The passengers were all volunteers and to create as realistic an exercise as possible for the participants, passengers had make-up to simulate severe cuts and bruising. Moreover, passengers had been briefed on how to behave and some added a further degree of realism by not cooperating with their rescuers.

"Our ambulances carried skilled teams from MDH and some from abroad, which goes to show people are coming here to Malta to learn from the skills of those who are needed to save lives in a crisis." (Hook, 2013)

There were no flight arrivals or departures scheduled during the exercise, although had a real emergency occurred, the airport would have been closed and aircraft redirected to nearby airports, such as Catania in Sicily. Times of Malta journalist, Kristina Chetcuti observed:

"Everyone seamlessly followed the routine and behaved as they would in the event of an actual accident – except for members of the media, who of course would in real emergencies be kept as far away as possible from the accident scene." (Chetcuti, 2013)

However, as one off duty senior fireman told me, they decided to locate the rescued passengers downwind of the fire which was not a shrewd move.

The exercise was being closely assessed by a number of transport representatives and as Head of Airport Communications, Reuben Sciberras, revealed:

> *"They need to ensure that all the International Civil Aviation Organisation's regulations are being adhered to, not just the timing (of the exercise) but also the procedures"* (Chetcuti, 2013)

6.4 Rehearsing a 9/11 type scenario 16 years before it happened

Scenario

This exercise simulated a multiple incident that included denial of access, loss of key staff and explosion leading to fire. We read about 'designer disasters' but in this particular situation just about anything that could go wrong was included as part of the exercise. The scenario selected was that an aircraft crashed into the organisation's premises, destroying the building and killing/injuring half of the employees. It could have been a terrorist attack or just an aviation accident.

The killed/injured employees were selected at random which meant that some key members of staff were not available to support the business recovery.

Simulated duration: Two days

Detail

World War II saw the dawning of the Kamikaze, with its inherent acts of self-sacrifice. Japanese pilots crashed their aircraft into Allied warships in a desperate effort to inflict catastrophic damage on the vast naval capability ranged against them. Fast forward 40 years and terrorists began to adopt self-sacrifice tactics, or suicide bombings, as a means of targeting their victims. The first terrorist suicide attack that received worldwide attention was in Beirut on 23 October 1983. Around 300 US and French troops were killed when their barracks were targeted (Kiras, 2014). Fast forward another 18 years to 2001 and the world witnessed the horrific and calculated attacks on the World Trade Center and the Pentagon. This time the suicide bombers emulated the Kamikaze model and flew hijacked planes into their intended targets. The rest, as they say, is history.

On reflection, it now almost seems somewhat prophetic, but 16 years before 9/11, I was involved in a business continuity rehearsal for a self-contained part of an organisation. The chosen scenario was that a plane crashed into the building killing around 50% of the staff. The exercise was looking to establish whether, given the circumstances (denial of access and loss of key staff, etc.), the business could recover from the incident.

"The graveyards are full of indispensable men."
Charles de Gaulle

So how was this accomplished? First, the participants were instructed to attend a briefing the following day, although the reason was not disclosed, effectively making this an unannounced exercise. At the briefing they were informed of what was happening, the selected scenario and the objectives of the day. This was followed by the random selection of 'victims', using a fairly basic form of random absentee modelling. Each of the participants was invited to select a sealed envelope and inside was a message informing them whether or not they were a victim. It is kismet that dictates when any of us are in the wrong place at the wrong time and we suffer the consequences accordingly. Some of the '*victims*' were experienced key members of the team. However, there were no exceptions made. If they had 'succumbed' then they were not permitted to take any part in the rehearsal. While they were allowed to carry on with their respective day jobs, should anyone have attempted to solicit any recovery flavoured advice from them, victims were instructed to tell them "*Sorry, I'm dead – can't help you*".

Though it was acknowledged that the simulated loss of key personnel slowed the recovery process, the business continuity plan worked and the primary objective was successfully achieved. 9/11 aside, there are many other instances of aviation accidents around the globe with planes crashing into buildings. Even so, you may argue that, unless your premises are directly under an airport flight path, and assuming you are not based in a highly prestigious or symbolic building that terrorists might choose to target, the probability of being a casualty of such an incident is very low. However, the circumstances of the disaster scenario selected could have been very different, while the end result was very similar. For example, an explosion, a fire, a toxic chemical release or a pandemic, could each decimate a workforce. Moreover, do not assume that because someone is not physically hurt that they will be capable of supporting a recovery, as they may have been traumatised by the incident and possibly be incapable of working. You should also keep in mind that the effects of trauma can last for extended periods. In the case of the 1996 IRA bombing of Manchester, some people were still being counselled for trauma more than

6: Live Rehearsal Case Studies

two years later, even though the area threatened by the bomb had been evacuated (Tehrani, 2004).

In the publication '*In Hindsight – A Compendium of Business Continuity Case Studies*', one chapter is dedicated to the recovery of Northgate Information Services. In 2005 their headquarters was destroyed by a massive explosion in the neighbouring Buncefield oil depot, necessitating the relocation of the 500 plus staff and a full IT disaster recovery. Northgate were subsequently awarded the prestigious accolade of 'Best Recovery of the Year'. The organisation took its information services supplier responsibilities very seriously and had an ongoing rigorous testing programme. This included what they considered to be worst case scenarios, although this did not foresee a loss of key staff. Fortunately, the explosion occurred around 6 am on a Sunday morning and the building was virtually empty. One leading fireman attending the incident remarked that numerous fatalities in the Northgate premises would have been an inevitability had the explosion occurred during the working week. Acknowledging this, Northgate's Business Recovery Director, Mark Farrington, remarked:

> "*Had we lost any of the 30 core support staff that knew the systems best, we would have been stuck.*"
> (Clark, 2014, p. 43)

Rather alarmingly, I have often seen statements in business continuity plans which assume that all of the workforce will be available to assist with any recovery activity. A crucial message to take out of this section needs to be that you should never make such an assumption and you should reflect this in your BCP and its ensuing validation. Keep in mind that their absences may not be anything more sinister than the employees are on vacation, maternity leave, sick leave, Armed Forces Reserve training or jury service, etc. The list goes on. But if they are not available, then they are simply not available – learn to live with it!!

6.5 Sorry, you cannot evacuate the building before lunch is finished!

Scenario

The decision was made to run a live and unannounced test to validate the response to a denial of access situation. The organisation was property rich and one of its sites was selected, with the intent of establishing how well the plan would work if the building was closed for several days. The scenario was 'white powder' discovered in a package by post room staff.

This exercise was enacted by a large multinational organisation and it was designed to evaluate how well each of the involved department's BCP's performed. It was also an awareness exercise to see how individuals behaved – where would they go, what would they do and would they try and re-enter the building before the exercise was completed.

Actual duration: Three days

Detail

Broadly speaking, the original intent was to activate the fire alarm during the morning and evacuate the building. A morning was chosen as it was believed that employees based at the selected office would be less tempted to just go home when the exercise started. Fire drills were well-rehearsed exercises and staff would be expected to assemble at their designated fire assembly points (FAP) in the car park, unless given instructions to the contrary. Once mustered at their FAPs, they were advised that a package which contained an unidentified white powder had been discovered by the post room. The emergency services had been called and the organisation had been instructed to close the building with immediate effect. It was anticipated that the building could be closed for several days while the powder was analysed. A security presence was to be maintained to prevent any unauthorised re-entry.

The building selected did not house a data centre and so there were no IT disaster recovery implications incorporated into the exercise. However, rather than simply activate the fire alarm and evacuate the building as originally intended, employees were instructed to collect their personal belongings and laptops before heading for their designated FAPs. So in one sense, this exercise was bordering on the designer disaster, as the severity and potential risk to life and limb generated by some scenarios would demand an immediate, non-negotiable evacuation. Health and safety regulations would invariably dictate that the provision of a convenient window in which employees could collect their personal belongings, in addition to laptops and the like, was a luxury that simply could not be afforded.

Once staff had gathered at their fire assembly points, their names were recorded and they were then requested to follow the instructions in their department's BCP. As this was, in part, an awareness exercise, staff were later contacted and asked what action they took and why. Some went home as they could work just as well from there. Several indicated that they had gone to one of the organisation's other offices and based themselves there, as that was what their plans said they had to do. Others went and worked at their respective client sites, again in line with their plans. There were a small minority who had no idea what to do and at least one of them decided to go shopping.

In closing the office without prior warning, we had to make sure that we were not going to end up with '*egg on our faces*' in the event that the whole exercise went badly wrong. To reduce the prospect of such an occurrence, we undertook an extensive risk assessment exercise which threw up a number of issues that needed consideration. Some of these risks we decided to accept, however, there were two in particular that we could not leave to chance.

1. The building selected was also one that the organisation's clients could well be visiting for a variety of reasons. However, these visits were always hosted in a suite of specially designated rooms. To avoid any embarrassment, we reserved every room in the visitors' suite for the duration of the exercise, to make it difficult to entertain any clients during that time.

2. The second major concern was centred around lunch, of all things. While the executive management agreed the plan, they placed one caveat of particular note on the whole exercise. We were not permitted to start evacuating the building until the lunch break had finished. No they were not concerned about whether staff had had their lunch before they were sent off into the snow (Yes, it is had been snowing just before). The concern was that if food prepared by the catering company was wasted, someone would need to pay for this out of their budget. While the point was well made, I'm not sure if a real disaster occurred there whether it would be so accommodating on the timing.

6.6 Three active shooter situation exercises

"An active shooter is an individual actively engaged in killing or attempting to kill people in a confined and populated area, and recent active shooter incidents have underscored the need for a co-ordinated response by law enforcement and others to save lives." (FBI, 2013b)

The three case studies in this section each deal with universities exercising various aspects of their response to an active shooter scenario. Gun attacks targeting educational institutions and their students are nothing new and sadly they show no sign of abating any time soon. Many schools and universities present open soft targets which can only work to the advantage of the would-be mass murderers in maximising their heinous objectives. The problem is not unique to any one country and occurrences appear completely random. Active shooter attacks are usually the actions of a single gunman, although in the 2015 case of the Garissa University in Kenya where 148 died and 79 were injured, this attack was perpetrated by an organised terrorist cell. In a similar case in 2014, 145 were killed at the Army School in Peshawar, Pakistan.

One famous survivor from a school shooting incident was the British 2013 UK and US Grand Slam tennis champion, Andy Murray. Along with his brother Jaimie, he survived the Scottish Dunblane school massacre in 1996. A recently televised interview shows that the memory of that tragedy continues to haunt him to this day (Murray, 2013).

However, being on the wrong end of an active shooter situation is not solely the domain of educational institutions. Between 2000 and 2013 the FBI reported 160 gun related incidents within the US alone that resulted in 486 deaths, with a further 557 being injured. Moreover, while 24% of these attacks targeted the education sector, as many as 46% featured commercial targets (FBI, 2013). Outside the scope of the FBI report was the attack on Nairobi's Westgate Shopping Mall in 2014 which resulted in a four day siege, leaving 67 fatalities. Similarly, what has since become known as a Mumbai style attack, originally occurred in November 2008 when the city's Taj Mahal Palace Hotel was attacked by terrorist gunmen that culminated in some 167 fatalities.

National law enforcement agencies can usually advise on how to mitigate the risk of attacks while identifying measures that can be implemented to help improve the safety of students and employees in the event of an attack. Two such examples are the UK's National Counter Terrorism Security Office (NaCTSO) and the US Department of Homeland Security (DHS).

6.6.1 Scenario one

3 January 2014, the University of North Carolina at Charlotte (UNC Charlotte) exercised its lockdown system. Securing the campus buildings by implementing a lockdown condition is a computerised process. Its primary objective was to ensure that while building occupants could get out, it would not be possible to enter any of the university buildings, even with a valid swipe card.

Actual duration: 15 minutes

Detail

With no end in sight to the 'lone wolf' gun attacks at schools and universities, in the event of an emergency, the

Police and Public Safety Department (PPS) can initiate a computerised campus lockdown of all university facilities, including UNC Charlotte Centre City.

Although the author has not had sight of the results of the exercise, what is clear is that the university kept the 25,000 plus student population advised of events by using social media. Both its Facebook (UNC Charlotte) and its Twitter (@unccharlotte) accounts were utilised in the exercise (search on 'lockdown' on both accounts for further details).

As Lieutenant Brian Thomas from the Police and Public Safety Department (PPS) explained:

> *"Officials anticipate the test to take between 10 and 15 minutes to complete. At the conclusion of the test, doors should return to their normal operation. PPS conducts such tests throughout the year as part of the University's emergency preparedness program."*
> (Brown, 2014)

6.6.2 Scenario two

UNC Charlotte is not alone in exercising its emergency procedures and other universities are also testing their own. Dartmouth College located in Hanover, New Hampshire, is another point in case. On 23 February 2012, it tested its Outdoor Mass Notification System (OMNS) and involved not just the college but also the population of Hanover itself. The OMNS comprises of a combination of sirens and voice speakers that can be used to warn not just the college student of emergency situations but also local inhabitants. The system is so effective that it can be heard as far away as Lyme, approximately ten miles (16 km) from the campus.

In the event of a real emergency alert, in addition to activating the sirens, the OMNS can be used to broadcast an audible message that advises both students and local inhabitants to '*shelter in place*'. This acts as an instruction to "stay inside in one's current location, lock the doors, stay away from windows while awaiting further instruction" (Dartmouth College, 2012)

6.6.3 Scenario three

Ever since the 2007 Virginia Tech massacre, when 32 were shot and killed, with a further 17 injured, the Wayne State University in Detroit has made security a top priority. Substantial investment has been made in technology, along with several thousand hours of tactical police training, to prevent a similar tragedy occurring.

With a population of 40,000, the university takes crisis management very seriously, along with its commitment to maintain the safety and security of the campus community. In line with this level of professional dedication, 27 March 2015 witnessed the Wayne State University Police Department (WSUPD) conducting a mock active shooter exercise. While the FBI estimates that the average active shooter incident lasts only 12 minutes, this full day exercise commenced at 7 am and concluded at 4 pm.

Actual duration: Nine hours

Detail

Following the university launching the nation's first online training curriculum for civilian response in an 'active shooter' emergency in 2009, the March 2015 WSUPD exercise demonstrated that it was prepared to practise what it was preaching.

"These types of mock exercises require several weeks of preparation and co-ordination on the part of every member of our police department. The training benefit and deployment evaluation is valuable to the department as we strive to be optimally prepared to handle crisis situations." Anthony Holt, Chief of Police, Wayne State

Students volunteered to act out various roles and stage make-up and theatre blood was used to create the illusion of injuries and fake bullet wounds. To add to the realism of the exercise, police cars were used to block streets in the vicinity of the university.

With the anticipated concentration of heavily armed police, along with police vehicles and ambulances, local inhabitants were briefed about the exercise and told not to be alarmed. Moreover, they were advised that 'injured victims' would be evacuated from the scene and transferred to a mobile triage unit.

"This multifaceted simulation served as an excellent test for our police officers in a realistic and high-adrenaline drill. Evaluators closely observed our officers, beginning with the initial emergency call to our dispatchers and continuing throughout the scenario until the active shooter was neutralised and the campus area secured." Anthony Holt (Wayne State University, 2015)

To keep students and staff apprised of safety related issues, the university has a broadcast messaging service. It offers the option of receiving safety related text messages via their cell phones, although as a matter of course, alerts are automatically sent by email.

6.7 Waking Shark II – Desktop cyber exercise

With high-profile cyber attacks rarely out of the news, FBI Director, Robert Mueller III's 2012 prediction *"There are two types of organisation, those that have been hacked and those that are going to be hacked"* seems even more prophetic. It is hardly surprising that more and more organisations are turning their attention towards how best to protect themselves from this ever growing and mutating threat.

This case study looks at a desktop exercise organised by the Bank of England (BoE) called Waking Shark II which was similar to a large scale simulation that had been acted out earlier in the year in New York called 'Quantum Dawn 2'.

This was a big exercise and the scope included the wholesale markets, investment banks and the financial market infrastructures (FMI) supporting those markets, with the intent of evaluating inter-company communication, in addition to communications between companies and the financial authorities. In excess of 200 were drawn from numerous participating companies including Barclays, Royal Bank of Scotland, JP Morgan, HSBC and Goldman Sachs. They were joined by several FMI providers including SWIFT and CHAPS. Supporting expertise came from a number of sources including British Telecom, the British Bankers' Association, Centre for Protection of National Infrastructure (CPNI) and Cyber Security Operations Centre.

The BoE published supporting documentation and the various independent commentaries that both preceded and followed the exercise are voluminous. Consequently, this study has been restricted to a precis of the material available. However, if readers would like a greater depth of information, where appropriate, references can be found in Section 14 – Works Cited.

Both Santander and Barclays Bank had been targeted by cyber attacks earlier in 2013. While the Santander attack was foiled, in excess of £1 million was siphoned out of Barclays by the perpetrators. UK police subsequently arrested 12 men for the Santander cyber attack and a further eight in connection with the Barclays incident. With this in mind, it is curious that while the exercise involved BoE, HM Treasury and the Financial Conduct Authority, there was no law enforcement involvement, particularly as the scenario selected is a criminal offence within the UK.

"It is vitally important that cyber security tops the priority list for IT departments in the UK's financial service organisations ... Not only are banks operating with legacy systems that in some cases have been in existence for many years, it is also a sector where innovation across new banking channels, such as online and mobile, is creating complex multi-channel IT infrastructures." Dorian Wiskow, Financial Services, Fujitsu UK & Ireland (Ashford, 2013)

Ironically, with the cyber threat seen by many CIOs as the number one challenge, not only to ICT environments but in some cases to organisational survival, some may argue that ICT departments are having to deal with real cyber attacks so frequently that cyber threat validation may seem to some as a rather superfluous exercise.

Prior to the start of the exercise, the Financial Times quoted PwC's Richard Horne and his reference to another actual cyber attack on banks and broadcasters in South Korea earlier in 2013, for which Seoul pointed the finger of blame firmly at North Korea.

"The South Korea events have opened many peoples' eyes to what is possible." (Fleming, 2013)

Objectives

Keeling's post exercise report (Keeling, 2013, p. 3) states that *"The objectives focused on disruption/dislocation in wholesale markets and in the financial infrastructure supporting those markets as a result of a concerted cyber attack.*

The specific aims of the exercise were:

- *To assess whether firms had adopted the feedback and lessons learnt from Waking Shark I, which recommended that financial sector organisations should:*
  - ○ *review their internal cyber incident response procedures*
  - ○ *review their representation and engagement with the existing external crisis, security co-ordination and information sharing groups (e.g. CPNI, CSIRTUK, etc.) and*
  - ○ *assess the mechanisms in place to ensure that the external and internal information available would be leveraged in the event of a cyber incident.*

- *To exercise communication and information flows between firms, and between firms and regulators, during a cyber attack (as established in Waking Shark I), most notably:*
  - ○ *FSIE as a technical information sharing forum and by using the CISP platform*
  - ○ *CMBCG in the role of industry co-ordinator for such events.*

- *To improve understanding of the impact of a cyber attack on the financial sector and how the sector should respond, as identified by the 2011 MWE."*

Scenario

Keeling explains that the scenario was expected; *"to meet the exercise objectives a scenario was devised that placed the sector under severe stress. As such, the elements of the scenario were extreme relative to the cyber attacks that have been seen to date. The scenario was based on a concerted cyber attack against the UK financial sector by a hostile nation state with the aim of causing significant disruption/dislocation within the wholesale market and supporting infrastructure. Although the impacts caused by the cyber attacks would have had an international as well as a UK dimension, for the purposes of the exercise, the scope of the exercise was restricted to management of the UK impacts.*

The scenario was set over a three day period, the last day of which happened to coincide with 'Triple Witching' (when contracts for stock index futures, stock index options and stock options all expire on the same day).

The three day period was broken into phases, playing out various technical and business impacts from the scenario. The scenario examined how firms would manage their response to the cyber attacks both on a technical level (in particular information-sharing amongst the firms via the CISP tool), and from a business perspective.

The following technical and business impacts were included in the scenario:

- *DDoS attacks, causing the firms' global websites and certain other internet-facing systems to be unresponsive or intermittently available.*
- *APT and PC wipe attacks that penetrated the firms' networks for disruptive and destructive purposes.*

- *Issues with end-of-day market data pricing files for some equities markets, causing challenges with overnight risk and margin calculations.*

- *Issues with central counterparty clearing processes for fixed income, with resulting events causing significant liquidity and funding issues.*

- *Issues associated with processes used to instruct payments through agent banks and manage balances in accounts at agent banks.*" (Keeling, 2013, pp. 3–4).

Simulated duration: Three days but elapsed time was six hours

Detail

After an initial briefing, the exercise got underway with a simulated DDoS attack on the Bank's UK customer facing web presence, causing extreme bandwidth consumption to the detriment of all client facing portals.

During the exercise there were over 20 injects describing what the companies were experiencing. These were made up of primarily paper injects, along with TV media newscasts and Twitter feeds. In brief, the banks were experiencing:

- a massive distributed denial of access (DDoS) attack which was causing severe degradation of client facing online services, along with FTP servers

- an advanced persistent threat which analysis revealed had been in situ for at least two weeks

- malware had been discovered that uses a Windows vulnerability to pivot within the network. A patch had been available for several months but had not been installed.

The banks were experiencing a variety of consequential symptoms including PC BIOS failures and wiped disks. Moreover, significant corruption in closing prices and other data discrepancies had been detected. Something of a gloating tweet from a hostile fictitious foreign power was injected into the exercise telling participants that their systems had already been penetrated (please refer to *Figure 22*).

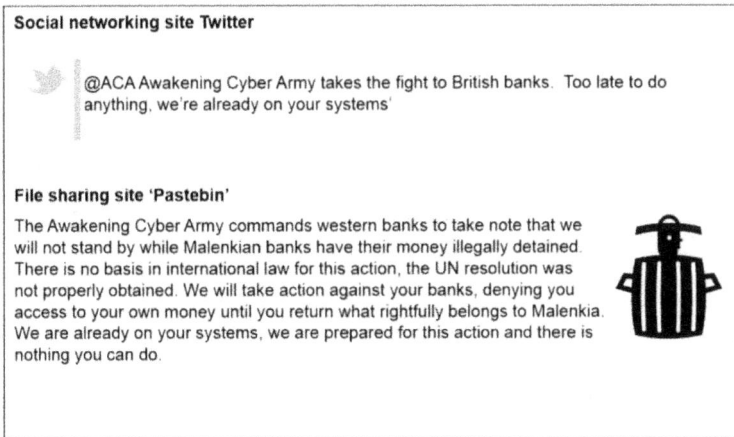

Social networking site Twitter

@ACA Awakening Cyber Army takes the fight to British banks. Too late to do anything, we're already on your systems'

File sharing site 'Pastebin'

The Awakening Cyber Army commands western banks to take note that we will not stand by while Malenkian banks have their money illegally detained. There is no basis in international law for this action, the UN resolution was not properly obtained. We will take action against your banks, denying you access to your own money until you return what rightfully belongs to Malenkia. We are already on your systems, we are prepared for this action and there is nothing you can do.

Figure 22: Waking Shark II – Exercise Twitter inject
Source: (Bank of England, 2013)

Advanced Persistent Threat Notification
Time: Exercise Day 1: 3:10pm

To: Security Incident Response Team
        Chief Information Security Officer

Notification from a cyber security company:

Incident Report

Advanced Persistent Attack Indicators

15:00

An Indicator of Compromise has been identified containing the IP addresses of several servers operated by a computer gaming company in the UK. The servers were compromised and used as command and control servers.

We have been assisting UK law enforcement for several weeks in relation to the servers.

Note: Your Information Security Team has just notified you that traffic has been seen from your firm's network gateways.

Figure 23: Waking Shark II – APT threat notification
Source: (Bank of England, 2013, p. 12)

PC BIOS Problems
Time: Exercise Day 1: 6:15pm

To: Chief Information Security Officer

Windows based workstations (all versions of Windows) and Operations workstations which have not previously been affected by the 'Blue Screen of Death' restart to a pirate flag styled bios splash screen provided by a replacement Coreboot bios.

The disks are apparently deleted and overwritten.

Approximately 10% of workstations are affected and the number appears to be increasing.

One PC matching the configuration of those wiped has been disconnected from the network for 2 weeks and remains unaffected. On inspection it contains custom malware that, when forensically analysed, contains the IP address identified as a command and control server used in the APT (Advanced Persistent Threat).

Figure 24: Waking Shark II – PC BIOS problems
Source: (Bank of England, 2013, p. 18)

TV News Bulletin
Time: Exercise Day 1: 10.00pm

The 'banking breakdown' is the main story on a number of news channels.

The Business Editor reports:

"...virtually every major financial website is down..."

"...chaos throughout the entire financial system..."

There is speculation on the loss of confidence in trading information, the effect on Triple Witching Day and postulation on the wider threat, and the cause.

The news bulletin ends with comments about what is to come:

"But the main question everybody in the financial world is asking right now is – how long before these problems get sorted? And is there more to come?"

Figure 25: Waking SharkII – TV bulletin
Source: (Bank of England, 2013, p. 23)

Conclusions and recommendations

Keeling reported that while some issues were raised, in general, exercise feedback from the majority of participants was positive.

But there are some other dissenting voices here as well:

	% age
Banks that considered that the scenario had been sufficiently challenging	44%
Banks who experienced communication and information sharing issues between other participants or with regulators	47%
Investment banks that had opted to initiate contact with law enforcement agencies	25%
Banks that had considered requesting a meeting with the Cross Market Business Continuity Group	8%

Source: (Davison, 2014)

143

While some cyber security '*experts*' acknowledged the value of the exercise and the derived benefits, others looked upon it as something of curate's egg – some good aspects and some bad points. Parallels have been draw with the need for the Critical Protection of National Infrastructure (CPNI), insofar as it could come under the same level of cyber scrutiny as simulated by Waking Shark II, with the potential disruption of essential services, such as the supplies of gas, water and electricity. Davison was especially critical regarding the detection of the APT within the duration of the three day simulation, as in reality it is likely to be a lengthy operation. He felt that this aspect of the scenario was naïve.

Specific recommendations came from four areas:

1. **Financial sector communications** where the findings propose that a single body should be mandated to manage cross-industry communications.
2. **Regulatory engagement** concludes that companies should be proactive in reporting major incidents to the appropriate regulator.
3. **CISP platform** should be further developed with the financial sector stakeholders working in conjunction with the government.
4. **Engagement with law enforcement** needs to be embedded in company culture such that reporting incidents to authorities becomes second nature.

"Waking Shark II has shone a welcome light on current vulnerabilities, but that doesn't mean it is safe to 'get back in the water'. Hackers see each barrier as a challenge to be beaten, meaning that constant vigilance and testing is vital if financial organisations are to remain secure." Stephen Bonner, KPMG (Leydon, 2014)

6.8 Wave I pandemic exercise

Introduction

Organisations preparing to face a pandemic need to appreciate that they are dealing with a threat to their staff and human resources departments should be primed to play a leading role. Moreover, it also presents a potential threat to both their customers and suppliers and could have significant implications on all aspects of an organisation's supply chain. Within the UK, pandemics have been classified by the government as a tier one threat to its security and it is ranked alongside terrorism, cyber attacks, natural hazards and military conflicts.

History tells us that we can expect pandemics to occur in the 21st century. However, we just do not know when they will strike, what precise characteristics that these contagions will present, or whether any particular sections of society will be especially vulnerable. But what we do know is that by their very nature pandemics are unpredictable and can have severe health risk implications. Moreover, they can come in waves with intervals of several months between each wave.

A number of pandemics occurred in the 20th century including Asian flu in the late 1950s and Hong Kong flu in the late 1960s. Between them it is estimated that more than four million lost their lives. However, this almost pales into insignificance when compared to the Spanish flu outbreak that followed World War I. Fatality estimates vary but many exceed the 50 million mark (circa three to five percent of the world's population) and up to 500 million were infected. Since the turn of the century, the human race has been threatened by Severe Acute Respiratory Syndrome (SARS), Avian Flu, Swine Flu, Ebola and Middle East

Respiratory Syndrome (MERS) among others. While tens of thousands of deaths have been recorded, we are yet to be confronted by the 'Big One', when we can realistically expect the number of global fatalities to be measured in the millions. Expanding the debate, one southern European country chief medical officer (CMO) that I recently had the chance to speak with at a seminar, expressed concern regarding the ever increasing number of immigrants trying to reach Europe from Africa. The CMO told me that it was possible that some of the immigrants could be carrying serious contagions for which European citizens may have no immunity.

"SARS was already spreading even before the World Health Organisation knew of its existence." (Feeney, 2014, p. 154)

What has become clear is that with global travel ever expanding and international tourism numbers predicted to reach 1.8 billion by 2030, organisations may receive little or even no notice of a pandemic heading their way. That said, many have already seen the 'writing on the wall' and have begun developing pandemic plans which are being incorporated and validated as an integral part of their business continuity management systems.

Scenario

The first wave of a life threatening and highly infectious mutant version of Avian Flu is rapidly proliferating around the globe. 77 countries have already reported infections to date. With the infection count rising at an alarming rate and the death toll mounting, the World Health Organisation (WHO) has declared that the outbreak has reached its highest classification level – 'Phase 6' indicating that a global pandemic is officially underway. A number of countries have already declared public health emergencies.

This validation case study looks at a London based mail order company that runs a 24/7 operation which receives around 70% of its orders via the Internet, with the remainder procured via telesales. Its crisis management team (CMT) has been convened and its pandemic plan has been activated. Although the exercise lasted only a few hours, the simulated duration covered several weeks. To add a degree of realism, the organisation's doctor had been invited to join the crisis management team to act as a pandemic subject matter expert.

This section includes only a subset of some of the activities that occurred during this exercise. In one instance, the 'clock' was advanced by up to four weeks. Even so, the study provides a substantial amount of data to reflect upon for organisations looking at their own pandemic planning arrangements.

Simulated duration: 12 weeks

Detail

Week one:

One of the first observations made by the crisis management team (CMT) was that the pandemic plan remained in a draft format and it had never been signed off. Even so, it was decided to proceed with the exercise and validate what was in front of them.

The human resources (HR) department informed the CMT that they believed that absenteeism was higher than normal for the time of year. However, as several members of the HR team had reported feeling unwell and had been sent home, it was not possible to provide a precise number at this time.

The company doctor briefed the CMT on how the pandemic was likely to develop, basing his comments upon both what was known already about the current pandemic, along with historical information about previous outbreaks. He warned that a pandemic can occur in a wave-like pattern, as illustrated in *Figure 26*, with the potential of several months respite between waves.

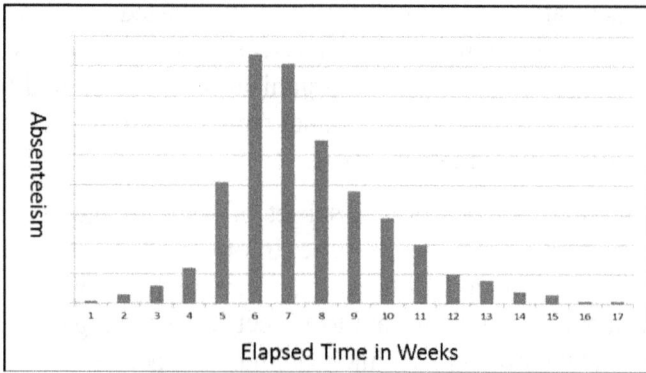

Figure 26: Likely profile of influenza infections wave over four months

At this time, the average recovery time that could be expected from the disease was unclear. Even so, people may well suffer with post-viral fatigue and not be fit enough to work for several weeks after they are no longer infectious. Even though many associated deaths had already been reported globally, no statistical data was yet available regarding the case fatality ratio (CFR). This indicates the proportion of symptomatic cases that result in fatalities. Estimations of CFR are particularly difficult to calculate during the early stages of a pandemic. But the doctor warned the CMT that based upon the table of historical data provided by the WHO (The WHO, 2013, p. 19) which is illustrated in *Figure 27*, fatalities within the company were a distinct possibility.

Pandemic year of emergence and common name	Area of origin	Influenza A virus sub-type (type of animal genetic introduction/ recombination event)	Estimated reproductive number (27, 28)	Estimated case fatality	Estimated attributable excess mortality worldwide	Age groups most affected (29)
1918 "Spanish flu"	Unclear	H1N1 (unknown)	1.2–3.0	2–3% (30)	20–50 million	Young adults
1957-1958 "Asian flu"	Southern China	H2N2 (avian)	1.5	<0.2%	1–4 million	All age groups
1968-1969 "Hong Kong flu"	Southern China	H3N2 (avian)	1.3–1.6	<0.2%	1–4 million	All age groups
2009–2010 "influenza A(H1N1) 2009"	North America	H1N1 (swine)	1.1–1.8 (31)	0.02% (32)	100 000–400 000 (33)	Children and young adults

Figure 27: Characteristics of the past four influenza pandemics

The doctor reminded the CMT that the sick bay facilities were very basic and had only one bed. It would be sensible to temporarily expand these to accommodate employees taken ill at work while arrangements were made to transport them home or to hospital. He also suggested that the company may like to look at ways of allowing staff to work from home if they have a pre-existing condition, such as asthma which makes them particularly vulnerable to influenza. He added that there are over four million adult asthma suffers in the UK alone.

He concluded his briefing by emphasising the importance of total compliance with all recommendations from the Ministry of Health, particularly with respect to preventing the spread of the disease. These are likely to include, although are not necessarily limited to, hand and respiratory hygiene, along with the avoidance of all unnecessary travel. Moreover, employees that use public transport have a greater probability of being exposed to the disease.

The organisation should also be prepared to accept that the government may encourage people to stay at home if they have come into contact with the disease but are not necessarily presenting any symptoms (e.g. one of their close family members has been diagnosed with influenza, etc.).

The pandemic plan had anticipated much of what the doctor covered and it included actions to identify which employees travelled to the London office using public transport, along with the creation of a list of employees who could work from home[5].

It was not clear how long HR would take to respond to this action as they were already short staffed. However, the HR director anticipated that absenteeism could rise during the pandemic for any one of a number of reasons including no access to transportation, fear of infection and illness. If the government decides to close schools, some employees may be absent while they are taking care of young dependants. Moreover, employees with infected elderly parents may also feel duty bound to provide care for them. The director also acknowledged the doctor's warning regarding potential fatalities amongst employees and advised the CMT that a counselling service had already been arranged for dealing with any resultant trauma amongst staff.

The administration director was asked to check if the company's business interruption insurance included pandemics, or was there some small print that meant they were not covered.

The CMT next turned its attention to identifying critical and non-critical business activities and each member of the

---

[5] There is no reason why lists of this nature cannot be prepared in advance of an incident or crisis as part of business continuity planning and then periodically reviewed. With the possibility of absenteeism rising, this is an additional task that could be avoided. This is also something of importance, not just for dealing with a pandemic threat, but for addressing other potential threats, such as transport strikes or terrorist attacks that affect the transport network.

CMT was tasked with drawing up a list for their respective sections. They were also charged with creating a list of those employees who were in non-critical roles but had the skills and experience to undertake a key role if required[6].

The final three decisions made by the CMT were that:

1. The company would immediately:
   - Replace the hand towels in the toilets with paper towels.
   - Sanitising hand gel dispensers were to be situated throughout the company's premises and employees would be encouraged to use them regularly.
   - Face masks and disposable gloves were to be made available for all employees, along with instructions for their use. A replacement supply was also to be kept on site for use when needed. All telemarketing staff were to be allocated their own personal headsets and they would be positively discouraged from lending their headset or using anyone else's.
   - A rigorous programme of sanitising stair handrails, lift buttons, door handles, telephones, computer keyboards, cafeteria chairs and tables, plus any other potential source of infection in the company's premises, was to be introduced with immediate effect. However, the building services director reminded the CMT that while he appreciated the importance of these additional measures, more staff would be required to undertake these extra duties.

2. All future CMT sessions were to be held using the company's teleconferencing facility, to reduce the risk of cross infection amongst the team.

---

[6] This information should already be available as a deliverable from the business impact analysis process.

3. CMT deputy members were to be kept appraised of all decisions and actions in case any of them needed to replace the primary CMT members.

Week two:

The building services director reported that he was having difficulty in sourcing sanitising gel dispensers and face masks due to the demand.

The CMT concluded that the critical aspects of the business that had to be kept running were the:

- Warehouse operation including upstream supply chain management, order picking and shipping
- Customer services
- In-bound telemarketing calls
- The payroll process, and
- The position on statutory reporting obligations was unclear and should continue unless the company was advised to the contrary.

All other activities would be performed on a best efforts basis and even though it would be disruptive, in a worst case scenario, these other departments could be temporarily suspended.

Preliminary figures were now available and it was estimated that around 79% of the workforce travelled to work using public transport. Some 12% either walked or cycled, and with the limited number of car parking spaces only allocated to disabled employees and the management team, very few used their own vehicles.

The ICT director said that the technology was already in place to enable customer services and telemarketing staff to work remotely and providing they had an Internet connection, they could work from home. However, some CMT members expressed concern that there could be employees who try and exploit the situation if they are not being constantly monitored by their supervisors. The director reassured the CMT that individual performance measuring software was now available, so each employee's activity could be remotely monitored. He suggested that they should be made fully aware that if they did work from home, 'Big Brother' would be watching.

Absenteeism was estimated to be 5% of the workforce. Randomised absenteeism modelling (RAM) was used to establish which employees were not at work and which departments were affected, although the reasons for each absent employee were not recorded[7].

The HR director agreed to communicate with staff on how working practices would be affected by the pandemic. Section heads would be briefed on the specific changes to their respective areas which they would disseminate to their staff.

Week four:

Absenteeism was now at 22% and the RAM approach dictated that two members of the CMT had been infected and had to be replaced by their deputies.

In response to a rise in customers enquiring about the status of order deliveries, the communications and media department are asked to prepare a statement which was to be issued via the company website and social media. When placing new orders, customers should also be

---

[7] While clearly needing to observe employment law, each organisation may well choose to adopt a different approach to absenteeism. While some may allow unpaid leave of absence (assuming employees are not actually sick) others may opt to keep them on full pay. For this, establishing the reasons of absenteeism could be important.

advised of potential delays. While apologising for any hold up in order processing resulting from the effects of the pandemic on the workforce, the statement should assure clients that the company will strive to ensure that orders will be delivered as quickly as possible. It should also reassure the clients of the company's continuing commitment to customer service.

The CMT decided to ease overtime constraints and section managers would be instructed to encourage staff to volunteer but there was to be categorically no attempt to pressure staff into working extra hours. The HR director warned against the potential health effects of working excessive overtime over a prolonged period. He proposed that a cap of 16 hours per week should be applied.

The outsourced ICT supplier contacted the company to say that staff shortages caused by the pandemic meant that they were obliged to activate the *force majeure* clause in the contract. They could no longer guarantee to meet the agreed service levels for incident resolution for the foreseeable future. This meant that any vital maintenance required to address failures in the company's online services, regardless of severity, could remain unresolved indefinitely.

In light of this, CMT asked the ICT director whether they should invoke their disaster recovery plan and transfer the ICT operation to the fall-back site. The director advised against this because at this time there would be no benefit as the service was still functioning. In fact, activating the disaster recovery plan could create unnecessary problems, particularly with the number of absent staff growing by the week. Moreover, if an outsourcing failure did occur, such as a software failure or a cyber attack, then it was possible that it could be replicated at the disaster recovery site.

The CMT learned that the RAM had also dictated that a member of the accounts department had died in hospital and a number of her colleagues were in a state of panic. The HR Director contacted the pre-arranged counselling service but was told that, at best, it would be several days before they could attend, due to their current case load.

The deceased was a young mother with two small children and the director was asked if he would be visiting the family on behalf of the company to pay his respects. He felt that as it was possible that her family could also be infected, he was not prepared to put himself or any other member of his team in a situation where they could be unnecessarily exposed to the disease. Instead, he would write a personal letter to the family and offer both his and the company's condolences. At this point discussions became very heated and the director's intentions were challenged, and he was accused of being totally heartless by one of his colleagues. But when asked if he was prepared to go instead and put himself, and possibly his work colleagues and his family at risk, the irate colleague apologised and backed down[8]. On checking, it also transpired that no next of kin contact details had been recorded for the deceased.

Week six:

Absenteeism was now at 43% and the RAM approach dictated that a third member of the CMT had been infected

---

[8] Here we face a moral dilemma – do we or do we not? Normally, many companies would want to show a caring side and support the family of a deceased employee. However, in this situation, by so doing they could put the health of other employees and their families in jeopardy.

and had to be replaced by her deputy. However, the deputy was also sick and, with no other suitable candidates available, the CMT agreed to absorb the missing director's responsibilities amongst the rest of the team.

Trains, buses and London Underground services were being frequently cancelled due to staff sickness. Many employees were arriving noticeably late for work. Warehouse activity was being especially affected.

With staff due to be paid this week, both the payroll clerk and her assistant had gone sick. No one else knew how the payroll process worked and there were no written procedures for someone else to try and follow – how will staff be paid? The HR director responded by advising the CMT that an agreement sanctioned by the chief financial officer had already been reached with the company's bank. Staff would be paid the same as they were paid last month and any appropriate reconciliation would be addressed after payroll staff had returned to work. This agreement would remain in place until the bank was asked to discontinue it.

A number of non-essential staff who were currently working at home had been instructed to report to the warehouse to backfill for absenteeism in that section. Three declined while four others demanded extra compensation because of the increased risk of infection they believed they would be subjected to, both at work and travelling to and from work. The CMT decided to consider their response.

The outsourced delivery company had not arrived to collect the orders ready for dispatch. When contacted, their office manager apologised and said they were short staffed. He assured the CMT that a collection would be made tomorrow.

Two more employees have died and the Evening Standard has requested an interview about how the pandemic is affecting the company and how it is rising to the challenge. After much debate, the CMT decides not to comment on the deaths and to refer the reporter to the statements already made. It was argued that after all it is only one of many organisations caught up in a common crisis[9].

Week ten:

Absenteeism was down from its week eight peak of 58% and was now back down to 31%. CMT opted to monitor the situation and react to any negative changes as and when they occurred.

Week 12:

Absenteeism is now down to 9% and the effects of the pandemic's first wave appear to be drawing to a close. As with week ten, the CMT opted to continue monitoring the situation and react as necessary.

Key lessons learned:

- Ensure that your plan has been completed, signed off and is regularly reviewed.
- Much of the work, such as creating lists and identifying critical parts of the organisation, should have been done in advance of this exercise as part of the BCM process. This is information that could be needed in a number of different scenarios and not just restricted to a pandemic.

---

[9] Normally I would expect a company to have a media plan in place and be able to issue meaningful statements and respond effectively to media questions. However, a pandemic is something that is likely to have a serious effect on many thousands of organisations around the globe and each could chose to react differently if they find themselves in the glare of the media spotlight.

- Items, such as sanitising gel dispensers and face masks, need to be procured before a pandemic starts, to ensure an adequate supply is secured.

- Sick bay facilities should be reviewed for suitability for temporarily accommodating staff who are taken ill on the premises.

- Both your upstream and downstream supply chain will invariably be affected by a pandemic, as will your customers. Employees of this particular company are also heavily dependent upon public transport to get to work, so any disruption to the transport network will have a detrimental effect on their ability to get to work.

- Human resources policies need to be carefully thought through. Due consideration needs to be given to how to deal with situations, such as requests for paid or unpaid leave, employees demanding extra compensation[10] or employees refusing to undertake certain tasks, as it may increase their exposure to the disease.

- Having a set of documented procedures available could make the difference as to whether an organisation survives or not, especially if you need to bring in untrained staff. In the case of payroll, while there were contingency measures in place, there could be a substantial amount of reconciliation work waiting for the payroll team to return to; work which could take some time to clear.

- Do not assume that because you have business interruption insurance that you are covered for pandemics – read the small print.

---

[10] If you make allowances for one employee and grant extra compensation, you may find it generates similar demands from other employees, so try and avoid creating precedents of this nature.

- Have a communications and media response plan in place, as they will be required for many of the situations that organisations may find themselves facing. Ensure you keep you stakeholders informed of the situation.

- Considering the delay for trauma counselling, unless you have an agreement in place for the provision of a dedicated service, you will have to accept that you will be competing with other companies for resources. Even then, counsellors can also become victims of the pandemic.

- Although this was a pandemic scenario, employees' next of kin details should be on record. Other incidents, such as fires or explosions that result in injuries or fatalities, even a simple accident at work, could necessitate the need to contact them.

Remember, this was only an exercise and yet the situation became very tense over the HR director's intentions of how to deal with the bereavement. Be warned, being in a real crisis situation can feel like being in a pressure cooker.

6.9 Twitter used in mock bomb threat exercise

Scenario

Both private and public sectors are frequently subjected to bomb threats, often which are nothing more than an elaborate hoax. However, to ignore any such threat would be irresponsible, as occasionally the threats are genuine. Sometimes, via an anonymous phone call, warnings are issued by the perpetrators, although this certainly cannot be relied upon to happen. Occasionally, suspicious packages are found which can also trigger a bomb threat alert. The media carries frequent reports of such incidents and an

Internet search using keywords such as 'London bomb threats' or 'New York bomb threats' will quickly yield an extensive list. Moreover, these lists represent just the bomb threat examples that have come to the attention of the media.

Although certainly not their sole domain, both hotels and airports appear to be regular victims of these threats. One hotel that takes bomb threats very seriously is the Europa Hotel in Belfast. During the Northern Ireland 'troubles', it gained the dubious distinction of being the most bombed hotel in the world, so its evacuation procedure was honed to near perfection. While the hotel was frequently damaged by bomb blasts, it never lost a guest or member of staff from an attack. Although two decades have passed since the troubles ended, the worrying rise of the threat from a dissident Irish republican terrorist element means the Europa Hotel maintains a high state of alert, while it continues to rehearse its evacuation procedure.

Moving on to the bomb threat facing the aviation industry, Canadian airports are required by federal authorities to conduct regular mock emergency exercises. This case study looks at a mock bomb threat exercise carried out in May 2014 at Edmonton International Airport (EIA), although in this instance the exercise trigger was the discovery of a suspicious package. The airport handled over eight million passengers during 2014.

I also heard a radio commentator recently suggest that an airport was nothing more than just a glorified shopping mall with a parking lot for motor vehicles and a second parking lot for aircraft. Maybe he had a point. So perhaps shopping mall security managers should also take note of this example.

Simulated duration: Several hours

Detail

The airport has its own detachment of Royal Canadian Mounted Police (RCMP) whose responsibilities include emergency preparedness training to respond to a range of situations, including terrorist attacks. In addition to its officers and civilian members, the EIA detachment also includes 'Badge', a five-year-old German shepherd trained to track and attack criminals, to search for lost persons and evidence, and to detect 15 different types of explosives (Edmonton International Airport, 2015).

The exercise commenced with the Canadian Air Transport Security Authority (CATSA) identifying a suspect item as a bomb and immediately notifying the RCMP explosive disposal unit team. They, in turn, worked with emergency medical service (EMS) responders, airport staff, and Badge, the police bomb detection dog. In all, the total number of participants numbered around 50.

The airport's daily operational activity was not affected by the exercise. Physically evacuating passengers as part of the activity was simply not an option, as the resultant disruption and the associated costs incurred, would have been enormous. It would also have had a knock-on effect on other airports, as aircraft arrivals and departures at EIA would invariably have experienced inevitable delays. Any interruption to operations can also result in airline crews passing the maximum time they can spend on duty which, in turn, can add a further layer of complexity to the situation. As one former international airport security manager told me *"Once passengers have had to be evacuated from the secure departure lounge area, you have no option but to process them all through airport security again which, especially at peak times, could take hours."* However, there is substantial material available from the live airport evacuations that occur periodically around the world in response to genuine emergencies which provide many valuable lessons to be learned across the industry. In fact, shortly before this exercise commenced, EIA representatives had been in the United States for a debriefing concerning the November 2013 shooting that killed a security officer at the Los Angeles International Airport.

> *"We like to learn from other people's experience and then we take those lessons back (to EIA) and apply them."* (Mainmann, 2014)

At Edmonton they have heavily and successfully promoted social media in the form of Facebook and especially Twitter. It is claimed that EIA has the strongest social media following of all the airports in the country and its @flyeia Twitter account has close to 20,000 followers. While the importance of using the local public address system in an emergency is acknowledged, there is also a firm belief that by communicating via Twitter at such a time could save lives. In fact, the social media site was used extensively during the bomb threat exercise to disseminate urgent messages and it is seen as a vital component in the airport's external communications strategy. Being able to quickly reach around 20,000 people is a very powerful addition to the communications tool box – which does not take account of the broadened outreach that re-tweeting can facilitate.

EIA has also found Twitter to be far more cost efficient and effective than relying solely on the more traditional call centre to respond to enquiries. In fact, the eight million annual passenger throughput equates to a daily average of around 22,000 – almost the same number as Twitter followers.

"Twitter really is a really popular way that people are trying to contact us now. We are somewhat unique in that respect, that we do have the strongest social media presence right now of any airport in Canada," said EIA spokeswoman, Heather Hamilton. She added that *"It's a definite shift we noticed in the last exercise and started to capitalise on in this one, where we would use Twitter more. When we're returning phone calls, if you're the sixth guy who called, it's going to be a while before you get that information."* (Mainmann, 2014).

6.10 Responding to a WMD incident

Scenario

This case study is primarily based upon information generally available via the FBI's own website (FBI, 2014). It is a good example of how government agencies work with the private sector and run exercises to raise the level of awareness of the real threat from terrorism. It also cites examples of how this has led to successful cooperation, in this instance between the FBI and private sector, that has unquestionably pre-empted and thwarted intended terrorist attacks. The FBI clearly recognises the importance of developing such relationships with the private sector as being an invaluable tool in the fight against terrorism.

This October 2013 exercise defined a situation that was considered to be a worst case scenario which witnessed the FBI Chemical Countermeasures Unit – part of its Weapons of Mass Destruction Directorate, lead a training activity in

Houston, Texas. It simulated a response to a weapons of mass destruction (WMD) attack, with the scenario being based upon the deliberate release into the atmosphere of a toxic chemical in Houston, Texas.

Simulated duration: One day

Detail

A set of procured chemical storage tanks presented a powerful visual aid during the exercise which had been primarily designed to rehearse the local emergency services in the preparation for a genuine chemical attack. The exercise extended beyond the local first responders to include Bruce Shelton, the facilities manager of a local hazardous waste disposal site in nearby La Porte. During the course of the one-day exercise, his company would experience a simulated break-in, a fire, plus the pilfering of a highly toxic chemical agent. This was just one of a number of high-risk chemical facility operators that the FBI was working with to alert them about potential threats in their areas.

The scenario dictated that the perpetrators intended to release the gas at a local waterfront amusement park, allowing a deadly gas plume to drift across the locality. This fictitious worst-case scenario exercise was devised by the FBI to highlight any weaknesses that might have existed in the area's sophisticated network of first responders. It also provided an opportunity for the two dozen local first responder's groups involved to operate in a cohesive manner.

One of the points I found particularly interesting with this exercise was that it was apparently also used to address questions, such as:

• Who has jurisdiction?

- Who is the lead investigative agency?
- Who is qualified to appropriately respond?

This left me a little surprised because as part of my Master's degree dissertation I had researched these very points with regard to the UK's own first response capability. Based upon the legislation contained within the Civil Contingencies Act 2004, what was clear at the time was that for a similar scenario in the UK (e.g. there has been a terrorist attack or an accident involving a WMD, etc.), the Fire and Rescue Service would take the lead role. They would also be responsible for any necessary subsequent decontamination measures. The ambulance service and paramedics would take on the role of triage and dealing with casualties, with whatever essential additional support that might be needed being provided by other health bodies. The police force would be expected to secure the area and gather evidence both during and after the incident.

Although it was not a WMD incident, I witnessed something like this first hand when I was evacuated from my office when the emergency services set up an exclusion zone due to a nearby factory explosion and fire at Aztec Chemicals in Crewe in the UK (Clark, 2014). Even though there was a real risk of ongoing explosions, they were prevented by the prompt action of the Fire and Rescue Services. Mercifully, there were no casualties on that occasion.

Meantime, returning to the case study, FBI Special Agent Amanda Koldjeski, a WMD coordinator in the FBI's Houston Division, remarked that – *"It's an excellent opportunity for everybody to get together and learn what each other's capabilities are."*

The waste disposal company's Bruce Shelton added *"As a manager you never want to be responsible for something like this going on. But I know that we absolutely need to be in contact with our local emergency planning folks in this type of environment, because we don't know what's going to happen tomorrow."* (FBI, 2014).

Shelton also acknowledged that he *"had never dealt with most of the individuals or agencies that participated in the exercise. Seeing the response unfold in front of him gave him a fresh perspective on his own role in securing his site and helping in a co-ordinated response"*.

Certainly one of the key lessons that Sheldon took away with him was that his company had a vital role to play in remaining vigilant and ensuring the site, and the hazardous products they handled, were kept secure at all times. However, in the event of a security breach, as in the exercise, it is companies like Sheldon's who are certainly best positioned to advise first responders of what has been stolen and how to deal with it.

6.11 Power failure – testing your generators

Scenario

Checking that generators activate when isolated from the mains power, thereby simulating a power failure, is a simple 'pass' or 'fail' test.

Please note that: most generators are self starters. By instantly kicking off when they detect a power interruption, they are very appropriate for providing a level of contingency against power cuts. However, there may still be a few older generators in use that will only start when connected to mains electricity supply. The latter generator models will obviously not provide the contingency required.

Simulated duration: Minutes

Detail

The Maltese Islands are renowned for suffering from frequent, unscheduled power cuts. About a year ago, I was there attending a meeting at a client's office. Both the CEO and the head of ICT were present when the lights went out. Two things then happened. First the lights came back on within about five seconds as a generator kicked in, and then shortly afterwards both the CEO and the head of ICT each received two SMS text messages. The first notified them of the power interruption, while the second advised them that the generator had restored power to the building. I commented upon the smoothness of the operation. With a note of sarcasm in his voice, the head of ICT replied by informing me that they used to regularly test the generator. He added that they had decided to stop when they realised that with all the frequent power supply interruptions, Enemalta, the local supplier, was doing it for them and not charging for the outsourced testing facility.

However, neither Mater Dei, the primary Maltese hospital, or Malta's International Airport, have resorted to this 'outsourcing' option and both regularly check their generators. Even so, each have experienced recent generator failures that followed national power supply interruptions. In November 2012, Mater Dei was reported to have been without power for four minutes, while a nationwide blackout in August 2014 resulted in the airport closure and re-routing of inbound aircraft for up to two hours.

Organisations that plan to use generators, or already have them in place, should keep in mind that they need fuel. You may feel that in saying that I am stating the obvious.

Moreover, if the outage is just a short term blip, then the generator and its corresponding fuel supply may well be sufficient. However, if the power interruptions result from an extended national or international fuel crisis (something that does happen periodically), getting replacement fuel for your generator may prove problematical. I cannot speak for other countries but in the UK if your organisation is not included on a government list as being vital to the national interests, you may not be re-supplied with fuel.

6.12 Bomb scare at General Hospital

In line with Home Office directives and their statutory duty under the UK's Civil Contingencies Act 2004, 14 May 2014 saw UK emergency services spring into action across the county of Sussex. Live exercises were conducted in the Eastbourne, Brighton and Mid-Sussex areas across two days. This was a large-scale exercise intended to test contingency plans in real time response and which took place in full public view.

Along with army bomb disposal experts and supported by other first responders and second responder services, armed police officers were summoned initially to the Eastbourne District General Hospital in a training exercise designed to assess their response to a vehicle borne improvised explosive device (VBIED) threat. The mock scenario simulated what was considered to be a major incident and the training was carried out in the vicinity of the nurses and doctors on-site residences. Organised to make it as realistic as possible, prior to its commencement planners did not reveal the exercise locations, to maximise the spontaneity of the event.

Code named 'Operation Citizen', the scenario was based upon an individual who was known to the police and was considered to be very dangerous. He was reported to have abandoned a suspect car before making his escape in a stolen vehicle. Conscious that the general public would have witnessed a considerable amount of 'blue-light' activity in the exercise areas, the Sussex Police Exercise Director, Steve Voice, remarked:

"Local people may notice considerable emergency service activity in these areas today. They can rest assured that far from having anything to worry about, this is actually a prudent test of our major incident plans and how we work with partners. It is extremely beneficial to the police and other agencies to test contingency plans, as directed by the Home Secretary, in a practical way and to continuously improve our service."

Steve Voice added:

"The scenarios we tested were exceptional and of a scale that tested our resources and provided very realistic settings at Brighton, Eastbourne and Slaugham Manor. We will be looking at the results of the exercise to see if there are areas of improvement that can be made to ensure that, should an event like this really happen, all emergency services work together effectively." (Eastbourne Herald, 2014)

Around 400 first responders participated, having come from close to 20 different agencies drawn from across Sussex. They were joined by some 200 volunteers who acted as suspects, victims and witnesses. The exercise continued the following day, with the focus of attention switching along the coast to Brighton.

"We are delighted to be part of this major exercise. We work closely with other emergency services on a

regular basis but – thankfully – incidents are rarely on a large scale. It is therefore vital we get the opportunity to experience different situations and test out how we can co-ordinate our response alongside other emergency services. We want to ensure we are effective in keeping those living, working and visiting this area safe." Glenn Jones, Group Manager, East Sussex Fire and Rescue Service.

6.13 No, Rakesh is an Indian

What a wonderful thing humour can be. It was certainly responsible for *'pouring oil over some very troubled waters'* and defusing a potentially explosive crisis management review meeting I was attending. It was a few years ago now and I guess there must have been ten or 12 attendees at this meeting. There had been a major ICT failure and, while it had been resolved, there was a lot of finger pointing going on.

One attendee came very close to dragging another attendee across the meeting room table by his jacket lapels. He was telling this department manager in no uncertain terms that he thought his entire team was nothing more than a useless bunch of cowboys. It was at this point that someone else interjected and said "No, that's not right. Rakesh Patel is an Indian". That throw-away remark generated guffaws of laughter that reverberated throughout the room and in an instant had had a totally calming effect on what was becoming an ugly situation.

My recommendation to you is that whether you find yourself in an exercise, or even facing a real crisis, when things become tense don't be too hard on someone humorous, as sometimes that can be just the tonic that the situation needs.

CHAPTER 7: IT COULD HAPPEN TO ANYONE, COULDN'T IT?

"Forget the adage about learning from your own mistakes. It's safer and more entertaining to learn from other people's mistakes!"

This section contains a series of accounts of BCP exercises that did not go quite as intended. Sometimes, the difference between success and failure can simply be how much attention you pay to detail. It is also certainly worth keeping in mind that if a live exercise goes wrong and you end up with a disaster of your own making, you may find that your actions have invalidated any business interruption insurance that you may have. Check with your insurer before finding out the hard way.

7.1 Did you hear the one about the Irish business continuity exercise?

We English are notorious for telling jokes about the Irish. In fact, our ability to raise a laugh at the expense of our Irish neighbours is probably only surpassed by their own ability to poke fun at themselves. However, this story is true and could happen to anyone.

This particular Dublin based organisation had decided to run a live exercise by validating a scenario simulating a fire in its head office. Picture the scene. The fire alarm was sounded and the building was swiftly evacuated, with the workforce assembling at their designated fire assembly points in the car park. A head count confirmed that everyone was out of the building, at which point the Chief Executive enquired *"So who has got the business continuity plan?"* The business continuity manager promptly replied saying *"I've got it, it's in my desk (in the burning building)"*.

Needless to say that this particular exercise went no further. But what can we learn from this rather embarrassing faux pas? Always ensure that you keep your BCP, along with any other vital records, in an easily accessible 'battle box'.

7.2 Don't forget to tell the emergency services

I first met the late Frank Emmanuel while I was still at school and he gave me a Saturday job in his Chichester jewellers shop at 29 East Street. Those familiar with this UK city will know that some of the buildings in this area are hundreds of years old and were certainly not built to the same safety standards that are applied to modern constructions.

A first floor room above the shop had been set aside for use by staff taking breaks. It was here that I noticed a very sturdy looking rolled up rope ladder bolted to the floor. When I remarked about my discovery to Frank, he explained that for a time, he and his family had lived in the apartment above the shop. Conscious of the potential fire risk and only one exit from the building, Frank had had the rope ladder installed in the room they used as their lounge. This was intended to be their alternative means of escape in the event of a fire. When I asked if they had ever used it he chuckled and then admitted that early one Sunday morning he had decided to put this escape route to the test. There was nobody around when he opened the window and threw out the rope ladder. The family was lined up ready to go and Frank's wife, Marjorie, led the way, followed by each of their three sons, with Frank bringing up the rear. As he reached the pavement he became aware that a small crowd of interested spectators had appeared out of nowhere. However, his attention was quickly grabbed by the arrival of a fire engine. A concerned member of the public had alerted the emergency services.

The upshot was that, while commended for his health and safety awareness, the local Fire and Rescue Service requested that Frank kept them informed of any plans for future exercises.

7.3 Your shortest RTO is two hours and it will take three hours to retrieve your BCP

One of the most important objectives for any exercise needs to be the verification that you can actually meet your recovery time objectives (RTO). I facilitated a series of exercise and testing workshops for an Italian organisation and what became immediately apparent was that its adherence to strict information security procedures was actually in direct conflict with its shortest recovery time objectives. Their almost paranoiac protection of their BCP was fuelled by the possibility of it falling into the hands of a competitor. Employees were forbidden to keep copies of the BCP on their laptops, or to take hard copies of the plan off-site, to mitigate the possibility of loss or theft. You may argue that their behaviour is not unreasonable given the level of sensitivity and confidentiality they attached to the BCP, even so, read on.

Their primary crisis management room was a standalone part of a hotel's business centre that was located approximately a 15 minute drive from their head office. However, the off-site battle box was kept at one of their regional offices, with a round trip taking approximately three hours. Had they needed to quickly evacuate their head office without having the opportunity of retrieving a copy of the BCP beforehand, the organisation would have little chance of achieving their most aggressive RTO of two hours. End result, a rethink on the location of the off-site battle box.

A slight variation on a theme can be found in Malta. Parking of cars in some locations can be notoriously difficult. In fact, I have come to the conclusion that vacant parking spaces have become something of an endangered species on the island, as there certainly seems to be more cars on the road than there are places to park them. One organisation's disaster recovery site was located in a town several miles from its primary data centre. During an IT disaster recovery exercise, staff used their own vehicles to travel to the DR site. What became apparent was that staff wasted valuable time in looking for parking spaces and without exception it took them longer to park their cars than it did to reach the vicinity of the DR site. The answer was simple – use taxis.

7.4 La piece de resistance – and I couldn't even claim the credit

In 2007, I was facilitating a crisis management training session in Paris for the local country management of a multinational corporation. The six hour session was scheduled to run from 8 am until 2 pm, where upon I was due to exit the building by 3 pm to catch a flight for an appointment in Portugal. However, the CEO requested that we delayed the start by one hour to which I agreed, although I reminded him that I had to depart no later than 3 pm.

The session got underway and made good progress. However, as 2 pm came and went, I must confess that I was keeping half an eye on my watch – not wishing to miss my flight from Charles de Gaulle Airport to Lisbon. Then at 2.45 pm, just as we were drawing to a close, something incredible happened. The fire alarm burst into life, signalling an immediate evacuation of the building. Aware that I needed to leave promptly, the CEO turned to me and asked "Did you organise this?". It was a brilliant end to our crisis management session and I would have loved to have been able to say 'Yes' and claimed the credit. But alas it was a complete coincidence, even though it did get me out of the building before my deadline. Maybe you can go one better and organise a fire drill and building evacuation as part of your crisis management rehearsals!!

7.5 Who has got the disaster recovery site key?

One client invited me to act as an observer for an IT disaster recovery exercise. It was planned for a weekend and the scenario necessitated testing the organisation's ability to transfer its entire IT operation to its fall-back site within the recovery time objectives. The organisation had already proved that it could recover all the key systems individually within their respective RTOs but they had never tried to recover from a multiple failure scenario.

The nominated recovery team assembled in a café opposite the fall-back site, at which point someone asked "Who's got the key?" It transpired that someone called Charlie had the key and he was on vacation and nobody had a spare.

On another occasion, although a different client, the designated key holder unlocked the door to the disaster recovery premises but, regretfully, no one knew the burglar alarm code, resulting in a visit by the police as the alarm triggered an alert at the local police station. It was some two hours before the alarm was finally silenced.

I would like to think that a simple desk check or a walkthrough would have picked up these two BCP deficiencies. But it did not. Both instances could have been easily avoided by attention to detail being applied during the planning for the exercises. Had either situation occurred in a genuine disaster situation, it would have resulted in far more than a few bruised egos and a large portion of egg on the face.

7.6 I'm sorry, he doesn't live here anymore

Keeping your contact details current is a vital BCM task and you should regularly ensure that any changes are reflected in your BCP. Although this example was strictly speaking not considered to be a BCP exercise, it was worse, it happened in a live situation.

It is confession time and I learned this valuable lesson the hard way almost 30 years ago. I was managing a team of IT techies trying to sort out a serious system failure and we concluded that we needed the specialist skills of a colleague who was not on duty at that time. Even though it was 3 am, his name was on the second level support list and so I duly telephoned him. When the phone was answered, I was horrified to discover that he no longer lived there. On reflection, I cannot believe what I did next. I actually asked the gentleman I had erroneously dragged out of bed if he had our man's new telephone number, which he politely gave me before bidding me goodnight. Needless to say, it was some time before I was allowed to forget that rather unfortunate faux pas, but rest assured I never did it again.

The problem we were addressing was classified as 'severity one' – just as bad as it could have got. Hence we were working through the night to fix it before daytime processing was scheduled to commence at 7 am. The financial cost of missing that 7 am deadline would have been huge, not to mention the reputational cost – both organisational and individual reputations were at stake. Thinking back, had the gentleman I dragged out of bed been less amiable and helpful, the sincere management gratitude that the team ultimately received for their overnight efforts could have so easily been management wrath instead.

Since that rather unfortunate incident, I have been involved in many desk checks and walkthroughs of client's business continuity plans. There was one that comes to mind, where I came across the contact details of various key supplier personnel that I personally knew no longer worked for those suppliers and in one case had not done so for several years. It is worth undertaking a simple and risk free exercise of actually getting in touch with the names on your contact list to verify that they are still valid, or that the telephone numbers haven't changed. It is far better to do this in a controlled and risk free fashion, then find out the hard way when you most need them.

7.7 Don't forget your desktop environment

I worked with an organisation to help validate their BCP which, at first glance, looked in reasonable shape. In the event that they were denied access to their head office, their contingency plan was to relocate the displaced staff across five other offices that were within a relatively short commute. This would have minimised the impact to the business while they either waited until they could reoccupy their head office or commission an alternative site, as necessary. Each of the five offices offered warm recovery facilities and had desks and chairs already in situ, along with networks. It was the intention to procure and configure PCs only in support of a live recovery situation.

In theory, the RTOs allowed sufficient time to adopt this desktop recovery strategy. However, a workshop exercise revealed that while their ICT recovery site had been well planned and constructed, they had not given nearly enough thought to the recovery of their desktop environment. With only one IT technician available to undertake the work, the BCP implied that he would be expected to work in five different places simultaneously. A tall order, even for Superman! Rather worryingly, it is not the first time I have come across this type of situation with insufficient attention to detail being paid to desktop recovery.

Now switching the train of thought to laptops, I would like to momentarily take you off on a slight tangent. Some organisations' policies concerning laptops are an interesting one. There are those that insist that laptop users must take their laptop home with them to pre-empt and avoid their potential loss in the event of a denial of access type scenario. Their business continuity strategies will often depend upon this happening. Yet, if you have to quickly evacuate a building because of a life threatening situation, health and safety considerations positively discourage you from taking anything with you, including laptops. The consequences of a denial of access happening during working hours could be that the PC/laptop related strategy is compromised. Food for thought perhaps?

7.8 We can't come, it's our Christmas cruise

With supply chains becoming more and more global and complex, effectively validating their resilience becomes much more of a challenge. For many organisations, their immediate suppliers, in turn, depend upon other suppliers, who depend upon other suppliers, and so on, hence effective *supply chain management* has increased dramatically in importance in recent times. The 2011 earthquake, followed by the devastating tsunami that ravaged parts of Japan, certainly underscored how global our supply chains have become. Industries that felt the impact included automobile manufacture and electronics and the launch of the iPad 2 in Japan was also a consequential victim of the tragedy.

Now it could be argued that stressing a supplier with unannounced exercises might not be appreciated by that supplier. But I probably don't need to remind you that genuine disasters usually arrive unannounced, and to make an exercise realistic, some of them should be unannounced too. With that in mind, a colleague of mine was organising a business continuity exercise that would require the support of a supplier. The supplier commitment was to provide a service 24/365 technical support for IT disaster recoveries and they were to be onsite at the organisation's fall-back location within two hours of notification of an incident. The contract between customer and the supplier also made provision for some unannounced exercises during the period of the contract. This was as much to test the state of readiness of the supplier, as to test the customer's own readiness.

It all seemed quite black and white. However, the agreement was put to the test one weekend, just two weeks before Christmas, and the supplier primary point of contact was telephoned. The news was not good. A rather embarrassed supplier manager explained that as part of their Christmas celebrations, the entire supplier company had only just sailed on a cross-channel ferry from the UK to France and they would not be back for two days.

Lesson learned – always check that 24/365 means just that. It is worth proactively enquiring about what arrangements a supplier has to provide support over a typical holiday period. Remember that disasters can strike at any time of the day or night. Moreover, they certainly do not respect traditional downtimes, such as national or religious holidays.

Now let's be frank about this. If there are no serious penalty clauses in a contract of this nature, then there is little incentive for the supplier to meet the agreed service levels, except to stand a better chance of being looked upon favourably when it is contract renewal time. For the duration of the contract, the supplier will be banking on not being called upon for either some form of validation activity, or to support a live incident.

While on the third party supplier theme, I can think of two organisations that have adopted similar strategies for replacing their desktop environments if the need ever arose. Both had a contract with suppliers that guaranteed to deliver the requisite number of PCs or laptops, etc., to the respective organisation's warm disaster fall-back site, within a day or two of being notified of an incident.

Now as I mentioned in *Chapter 3*, I once dropped my laptop and had to quickly procure a replacement which, because of where I was living at the time, was an easy undertaking.

However, this is not true of all parts of the globe and, at the very least, geographical constraints can sometimes result in lengthy supply chain operations. In some cases, even PCs are not 'off the shelf' items and have to be ordered.

I would categorise one of these organisations I have in mind as 'geographically challenged' and it was decided to put this desktop supply contract to the test, and one of their BCM team arrived unannounced at the suppliers. She explained that as part of an exercise they were conducting, she needed to have sight of the PCs that would be supplied in the event of a genuine incident. To her pleasant surprise, two things happened. First, the supplier showed her the first batch of PCs that would be delivered to meet the organisation's more acute recovery time objectives. Then, he produced a detailed plan of how the remainder would be sourced, including a delivery timetable. She left satisfied.

The second company that had adopted a similar PC procurement strategy had organised an exercise that necessitated the loan of 50 PCs for the duration of the activity. However, when the boxed PCs arrived, no one had given any thought about where to securely store them until they were required and they ended up being neatly stacked in the reception area. Security was less than impressive, along with a marked absence of CCTV. When the time came to deploy the PCs as part of the exercise, it was discovered that the 50 had become 41!

7.9 Who forgot to tell the catering manager?

While some organisations have 24/365 operations, for most nine to five type organisations, statistically, a serious incident is more likely to strike outside than during normal working hours. Consequently, contacting and mobilising the workforce may need to be done at night, over a weekend, or even during public holidays. Your communications plan should clearly indicate how and when the incident management participants are contacted.

Call trees (a.k.a communication cascades) are often found to be a method of choice, notably for smaller organisations. Although the function of this method of communication can be automated, some organisations still prefer to use a manual cascading information approach. For example, in the following diagram, George contacts Bill, Sue and Mike. Bill then contacts Roger, Ted and Peter while Mike contacts Claud and Jane. And so the cascade goes on.

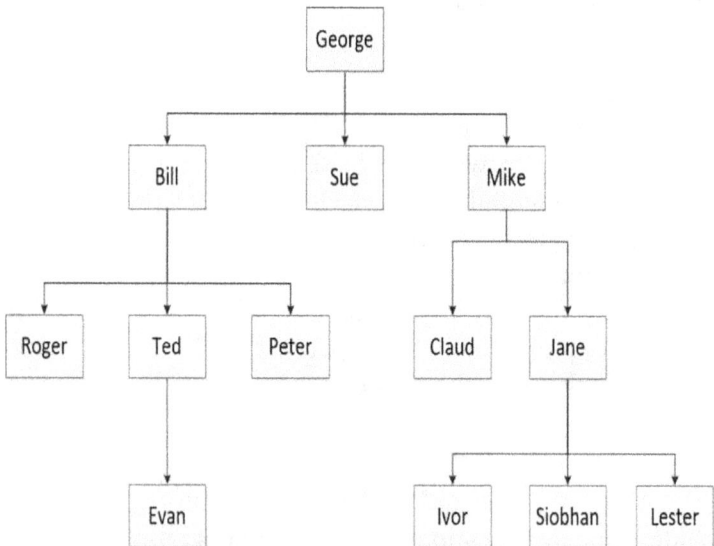

Figure 28: Communication cascade example

The exercise can also be used as an opportunity to establish how well prepared the call recipient is to respond to an incident, by asking them a brief set of simple questions, such as:

- Do you have a copy of the business continuity plan with you at home?
- What is the version number of the plan you have?
- Can you tell me what you believe you have to do now?
- Do you have a company laptop or tablet?
- Is it at home or in the office?
- Who do you have to call now?
- Can you confirm their contact details for me?

Exercises like this are actually multi-faceted. First, activating a call tree, whether planned or not, can help raise the level of business continuity awareness. It also provides the means of measuring how many employees could be contacted, and of those, how many had a current copy of the BCP, had their laptops with them and knew what to do next. When considering the objective of developing an organisation's state of awareness from 'unconscious incompetence' to 'unconscious competence' as discussed in *Chapter 1*, exercises like this call tree can provide tangible results. This is not a difficult or expensive exercise and can be repeated periodically, and the results will provide evidence of whether the level of awareness is improving.

Anyway, that is enough pre-amble, so let us get on to the case study. In this particular instance, a Middle Eastern hospital was participating in a weekend disaster management rehearsal involving all of the local emergency services departments, with the exercise being centred on the nearby international airport. The scenario involved the crash landing of a commercial jet airliner with several hundred passengers and crew on board. The hospital was expected to deal with the resulting 'casualties' and erect, and run, a mobile hospital based at the crash site.

As part of its own business continuity arrangements, the hospital had previously set up a manual cascading communication process. At the appropriate moment during the rehearsal, the communications cascade was activated. However, the chain broke, as the nominated individual responsible for notifying the catering manager, for whatever reason, did not make the call.

The consequence of this omission was that even though the rehearsal went ahead as intended, the hospital catering staff responsible for preparing and distributing food and beverages never turned up. The outcome was that none of the hospital's rehearsal team got fed or watered as they had been promised. This turned out to be a major moral dampener amongst the team which could have perhaps been avoided if the hospital had previously performed an independent test of the communication call tree to ensure that it actually worked.

The hospital's call tree was similar to the example featured in *Figure 28*. What was missing in the example was an action on the part of Evan, Ivor, Siobhan and Lester, where upon they contacted George to confirm that their respective activities had indeed been completed (see *Figure 29*). Had this approach been embraced by the hospital, the initiator of the call tree exercise would have known that the chain had been broken and could have taken appropriate action to deal with the situation.

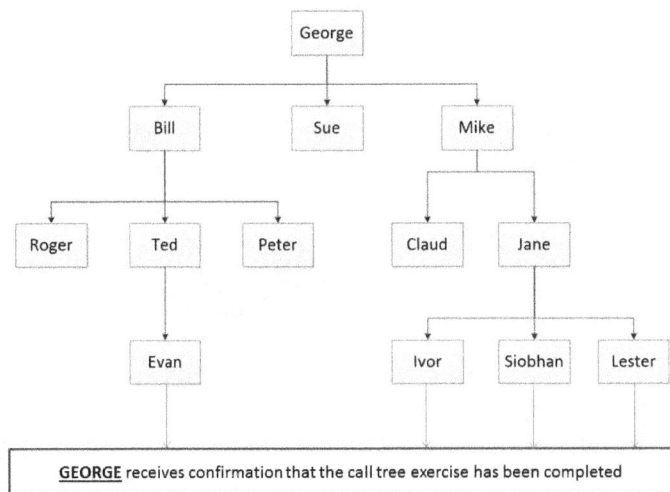

Figure 29: Communication cascade example two

Keep in mind that with both small and large organisations, a manually executed call tree chain can be broken by anyone for a number of reasons – the intended recipients of a call are on vacation, on sick leave, inebriation, their phone is turned off, or the battery needs charging, etc. Large call trees can also take more time to execute, especially if an organisation has to meet very short and aggressive recovery time objectives.

Chinese Whispers is said to have turned the message – *"Send reinforcements we are going to advance" into "Send three and four pence we are going to a dance"*.

When George initiated our example call tree, he will invariably have had a message that he wanted cascaded through the tree. By receiving feedback, George will also be able to have assessed how accurately the message had been communicated through the tree. He should have quickly become aware of any 'Chinese Whispers' situations that could have potentially compromised his original message.

While manually operated call trees may be simple and appropriate for SMEs, they are hardly practical when large numbers of employees need to be quickly mobilised to respond to an incident. In such situations, adopting a mass notification system, of which there are a number of efficient commercially available offerings, would be a sensible option to consider.

7.10 Check the small print in the contract

No names, no pack drill but I know of a large Dutch company with an international reputation that outsourced its ICT operation. What they failed to realise was that the contract they signed, while it did include data backup, it did not actually include any disaster recovery facilities. What is more, they never conducted a comprehensive set of disaster recovery exercises, otherwise this gaping hole in their business continuity arrangements should have come to light. It was only found when they actually experienced a major disaster and lost their primary premises, including their data centre. Fortunately, the company was big enough to absorb the impact – but at what cost!

7.11 Oh, we did a full live exercise of our BCP last Monday

While supporting a business development initiative, I contacted a prospective company to see if there was anything that we could help them with within the BCM consultancy services arena. Before calling, I had researched the company and knew that it employed in the order of 1,200 staff, spread across five UK based sites. I also noted that two of the sites were located on the same industrial estate and shared the same postcode.

I was connected to the individual responsible for BCM. After introducing myself and going through my opening gambit he quickly told me that they didn't need any assistance, as they had successfully validated their entire BCP only last Monday. After I had put the phone down, I thought about what he had said for some time. My gut feeling was that the bullshit monitor had just rocketed off the scale at the wrong end. So why didn't I believe him? I guess there are several explanations, any one of which could be appropriate. For example:

- He may have not been interested and just wanted to get rid of me. Fair enough, although why not just say so.

- Perhaps he was of the old school that still thinks that business continuity is just an ICT problem and they had checked that their IT disaster recovery arrangements met their recovery time objectives.

- It is conceivable that the exercise he was referring to was a desk check, although he had implied that it had been a full scale live rehearsal.

- Maybe the scope of their BCP does not cover the entire company, along with its products and services, which possibly did not leave much to test. Perfectly acceptable.

- It is conceivable that the most urgent of the company's MTPDs can be measured in weeks, or months, rather than in days or hours. In this case, they will have almost certainly opted for the 'do nothing' business continuity strategy because they have the luxury of time to decide on how to respond to an incident after it has happened. Once again, perfectly acceptable. But potentially there would be nothing actually evaluated, if this was indeed their strategy.

But let us assume, for the sake of argument, that they had a BCP that reflected a maximum tolerable period of disruption and the corresponding recovery time objectives that were measured in a matter of days or perhaps a couple of weeks. For the size of the company and for the nature of its business, to try and conduct a live exercise that validated your entire BCP, could be bordering on the foolhardy. One of the most important lessons for organisations to learn is that to try and exercise your entire BCP in one session is likely to be totally impractical, even when conducting a simple desk check. However, the whole thing could be fraught with danger, especially when you are conducting a live exercise.

Think about that for a moment. This outfit could have been trying to simultaneously validate plans by running a live exercise that was perhaps expected to deal with an:

ICT disaster recovery alongside:

- A long term head office denial of access simultaneously with.
- A pandemic that decimated the workforce not to mention.
- A product recall that was being hampered by a serious supply chain failure while.
- A category '5' hurricane was at full throttle pounding their premises with wind speeds gusting at close to 200 miles per hour (320 kph) and all this time.
- They were trying to fend off a distributed denial of access cyber attack.

Who knows what other scenarios they may have been concurrently addressing? And all this validation was performed on the Monday before my phone call – somehow I don't think so.

So if, as I originally suspected, the bullshit monitor was off the scale, then there was no harm done. However, if the gentleman in question was being honest, then on the one hand I owe him an apology. But conversely, the worry is that somewhere along the line his organisation has completely missed a very important point which could have cost them dearly, by unnecessarily exposing their production environment to the dangerous risk of a self-inflicted disaster. Had this happened, I am sure that their insurers would have been less than impressed and any business interruption insurance cover that was in place may well have been rendered invalid!

CHAPTER 8: MAINTAINING YOUR BCMS

"How long do you think your good plan will remain relevant for?" – (Wood, 2012)

Wood asks a very pertinent question because, in reality, the answer is that your BCP will never actually be finished. It does not matter how good your BCP is, or how much attention to detail that has been paid, it will continue to evolve to reflect the ongoing changes that every organisation will inevitably undergo. The only difference between organisations is arguably the rate and scale of the change that is experienced. As one business continuity manager once cynically told me – *"If the ink has dried on the plan, it is already out of date"*. Cynic or not, he was more or less correct. However, it is a sad fact that many organisations overlook, or even choose to ignore, the fact that business continuity management is an ongoing holistic process. I have personally seen BCPs that have not even been looked at for years, and if they were called upon as the basis for a response to an incident, likely as not they would be useless.

Once the plan has been 'completed', some act as though their BCM activities are now finished and believe they can turn their attention to other priorities which they consider more pressing. Resources involved in the BCM development are reassigned to other work. On this theme, very recently, I was made aware of a BCM manager being made redundant because his employer argued that, with the BCP now in place, his role had disappeared.

8.1 Maintenance activities

Maintaining your BCM programme is one of the three components of the validation process. By embracing it, it helps organisations to ensure their BCM arrangements are kept up to date and fit for purpose. The BCI's GPG identifies the following five maintenance activities:

1. Lessons learned through exercising
2. Changes in the environment in which the organisation operates
3. A review, particularly an audit
4. A real incident, when lessons learned can be incorporated
5. Updated or changed BIA outputs.

I believe that most of these activities speak for themselves. However, as the BCI's GPG does not actually spell it out, personally, I like to think that 'changes in the environment in which the organisation operates', incorporates keeping a watchful eye on developing threats. Let us face the fact that we are living in an ever changing world. Threats are evolving which business continuity managers need to take on board and subject to a thorough risk assessment process. Some of the more notable threats that have come to the fore in recent times have included pandemic, cyber attacks and adverse weather. I recently attended a conference where one speaker told the audience that every day, it is estimated that over 300,000 new cyber threats are launched into cyberspace. If accurate, that is an alarming statistic. You will recall that in *Chapter 3* I referred to the 30,000 Scottish inhabitants who had been without power for three days. We are certainly experiencing more and more adverse weather in the UK and we are told by weather experts that we should expect this to become the norm.

8.2 Keeping abreast of organisational changes

Maintenance needs to be embedded within an organisation and become a way of life. While the business continuity manager should be on top of the lessons learned from exercises or actual incidents, along with the output from reviews, etc., he/she may have no visibility of changes made within an organisation from both a business and technology perspective. This can make the challenge of maintaining the BCP more complex. However, those organisations that follow IT for service management (ITSM) best practice or the information technology infrastructure library (ITIL) as it is sometimes called, would find it a comparatively easy task to incorporate BCM within its change control process, thereby keeping the BC manager in the loop. Information coming out of the change control process could be fed into the BIA process as appropriate.

8.3 Project control

If you look upon maintenance as a project within the BCM programme, like any other project it will need controlling or managing. I would recommend that you do two key things:

1. Create and publish a project schedule which, as a minimum, identifies the tasks to be undertaken, who is responsible for each task, the expected completion and any critical path considerations that must be accounted for. Using a paper based plan may be sufficient but in which case I strongly recommend that you use pencil and always have an eraser handy. Personally, for ease of creation and maintenance, I would be more inclined to use a software based project management tool if one is available.

2. As a project manager, I always used the approach that if I was not getting progress reports from any members of my team when they were due, it would invariably mean some form of trouble – no news usually meant bad news. At the very least, I would find that they were behind schedule. I recommend creating and distributing regular reports to all relevant parties to keep them apprised of the project's status. Again, this does not need to be complicated and could include:

- Date of progress report
- Tasks currently in progress
- Tasks completed this period (could be weekly, monthly or whatever time period is appropriate)
- Tasks not completed to plan plus reasons for delay
- Action required to get back on plan (if appropriate)
- Tasks due to start in next period
- Issues arising (e.g. loss of key resource due to sick leave or jury service, etc.).

8.4 Managing your documentation

Finally, I would like to complete this chapter by raising something of a bugbear of mine. It is a concern which actually affects all aspects of business continuity management – document management and control. That said, I think this is as good a place as any to raise the subject. I was facilitating one exercise workshop and on a separate occasion observing in another when the same issue arose in each. Team members in both events had different versions of the BCP that they should have been referencing. In one of the sessions involving six attendees, there were three different versions of the documentation. How can this happen?

Well first and foremost, someone needs to be given the responsibility of document management – let us refer to this as the document coordinator. Now, if your organisation has an electronic DM system that will make your life much easier, but only if you use it. Maintaining a version control of all your BCM documentation (e.g. BIA, risk assessments, strategies, BCPs, exercise plans and results, etc.) is vital. However, keep in mind that once a document has been printed, it is no longer a controlled document.

The document coordinator needs to ensure that updated copies are distributed to the relevant parties, in addition to a copy replacing its predecessor in the battle box. To help you in maintaining effectual version control, it is also worth using a standard document format that has a document control page (usually following the header page). Typically it would look something like the following:

- **Document title**

  Acme Joke Company – Business Continuity Plan

- **Document reference**

  AJC Business Continuity Plan Version 2.4.docx

- **Document type**

  Business Continuity Plan.

- **Security classification**

  Company Confidential

- **Synopsis**

  Include a brief description of what the document is about

- **Document control**

Author	Document owner	Distribution controller
Alan Brown	Peter Grey	Sue Green

- **Authorisation**

Approval authority
Signature/Date
Jennifer Black, Director of Business Continuity

- **Modification history**

Version	Modification date	Comments
1.0	N/A	Pre-exercise plan
1.1	11/02/2014	Reflects results of walkthrough, 31/01/2104
1.2	23/06/2014	Plan revised following merger with LOL Novelty Company

- **Proposed next review date**

22/06/2015

- **Acknowledgements**

None

- **References**

None

Document coordinators must also ensure that the potentially more dynamic data required as part of the BCP, is kept up to date (please refer to section 7.6 for the one occasion I didn't). You can expect this data to reflect:

- Lists of employee contact details including out of hours contact details.
- If appropriate, lists of staff rotas.
- List of employees' next of kin and where and how they can be contacted (this information may well be managed by an organisation's human resources team).
- Contact details for suppliers that may be required to support a recovery. It would also be helpful to be able to reflect on what contractual agreements are in place, along with service level agreements, etc. For example, will the supplier be available 24/365 or is it only standard office hours, etc.?

CHAPTER 9: REVIEWING YOUR BCMS

9.1 Introduction

Perhaps the good news for SMEs is that the BCI endorsed book *BCM for Dummies* makes no mention of reviews, implying that the authors do not expect SMEs to conduct them. Personally, I do not think that reviewing your BCMS, regardless of how big or small the organisation happens to be, is actually a bad thing to do – it will certainly do you no harm and will invariably be of benefit.

ISO22398 barely mentions reviewing and ISO22301 covers its internal auditing aspects, whereas the BCI's Good Practice Guidelines devote more than five pages to the entire topic. The latter identifies the following types of reviewing:

9.1.1 Quality assurance

Quality Assurance (QA) I have talked about at length in Section 2.6. But to reiterate the key message, QA needs to be performed throughout the entire BCM lifecycle and not just left to the validation phase. Build resilience into your BCMS from the start, don't just try and leave to the validation phase – it does not work!

9.1.2 Auditing

The audit process which can be both an internal and an external process, evaluates an organisation's BCM programme compliance against a pre-defined set of standards, such as good practice guidelines or ISO22301. It validates that the BCM process has been followed, although provides no commentary with regard to its accuracy or quality.

The process will highlight shortcomings and auditors will expect these to be addressed, particularly if the audit precedes the awarding or renewal of an international certification.

9.1.3 Self-assessment

Self-assessment is an appraisal of the organisation's BCM programme carried out by itself and will look at how effectively the BCM programme is being operated. It will consider such things as:

- The status of scheduled plan reviews.
- Exercise programme: progress against plan and budget.
- Number of response teams members, and their deputies, who have taken part in exercises per year.
- Quantification of lessons learned and the number of action resolutions against plan.

9.1.4 Supplier performance

Supplier performance is a review of a key supplier's BCM programme. They may provide products or services on a regular basis, or possibly recovery services, or both. For those suppliers whose contracts may have been in place for several years, there may have been no provision made for the inclusion of any business continuity related clauses. However, for any new or renewal contracts, it is in the best interest of the organisation to ensure that the supplier provides sight of their BCM arrangements. Some organisations even insist that suppliers must have ISO22301 accreditation before they will entertain any key relationships.

CHAPTER 10: PERFORMANCE APPRAISAL

"He who stops being better stops being good." –
Oliver Cromwell

I am yet to come across two organisations that operate an appraisal and counselling process in exactly the same way. However, in general, it is true to say that the performance appraisal is a valuable human resource management activity which is intended to evaluate what an individual has achieved across a pre-defined measurement period (e.g. typically 12 months, etc.). It documents how well they have performed in a given role with its inherent responsibilities, against a set of pre-agreed tangible objectives. The results of the appraisal will invariably be used as input criterion for assessing individual pay awards, bonuses and promotions. Ideally, an individual's performance will have been informally monitored over the review period, with regular feedback being given as appropriate. This should result in there being no surprises in store at the formal appraisal meeting.

Performance counselling is a very important activity that helps employees to know themselves better. It should enable them to better understand their strengths and weaknesses. They should also be given feedback about their behaviour that should enable them to improve their professional and interpersonal competence. Another of the key outcomes should be that the appraised individual should leave the review knowing what their management considers that they did well and where they have room for improvement. Finally, the process should set goals for the next appraisal period and formulate action plans for further improvement. With respect to what I would call mainstream business continuity roles and responsibilities (R&Rs), these should have been defined within the policy and programme management practice, as described by the BCI's GPG. The measureable objectives can be quantified for those individuals once their respective R&Rs are in place. It is quite possible, particularly for SMEs, that BCM will only be a part of some individual's R&Rs.

There will also be those individuals who I would call fringe players and may only be required to be involved for very discrete business continuity activities, such as supporting part of the validation process. Even so, their cooperation could be of paramount importance to the success of the exercise and consequently their commitment is vital. Alas, some of those individuals may be reluctant to buy-in to the process and may need some form of encouragement (i.e. measurable objectives that effect their pay and rewards, etc.) to help them focus their attention on the importance of BCM. They may claim to be too busy, find they have a convenient dental appointment, or whatever other excuses they come up with for not supporting BCM as needed. These people need those measurable business continuity objectives to be in place unquestionably, even more than those employees involved in the mainstream BCM roles and responsibilities.

CHAPTER 11: USING CONSULTANTS TO HELP YOU EXERCISE

As an approved Business Continuity Institute instructor, I have frequently run the BCI's certificate course (please see section 12.1). At the end of courses, I have often been asked "So what do we do now?" The reality is that taking the academic experience and then applying it in the real world, can be a little daunting and this certainly applies to validating your business continuity plan.

Some organisations employ qualified and experienced business continuity professionals as a permanent member of their staff. However, for those organisations that cannot justify the ongoing expense, it can actually be cost beneficial to use a consultant to get you started and to make sure that you are heading off in the right direction.

The length of time an organisation needs a consultant will vary and will be primarily driven by how confident it feels about both the work in hand and the scope of their validation programme. But having an experienced pair of hands on board will usually help you get moving much faster than if you put together your validation programme on your own. However, it is important that the consultant does the work with you and not for you. In other words, when the consultant finishes the assignment and walks away, your organisation feels that it has complete ownership of all that has been achieved.

CHAPTER 12: TRAINING AND EDUCATION

In 2014, I was delivering a business continuity module to a group of postgraduate students who were reading for a Master's degree in Tourism. Most of the students were particularly keen to engage in the topic and one asked about further academic learning opportunities in BCM. Before my next session with this group of students I prepared the diagram below.

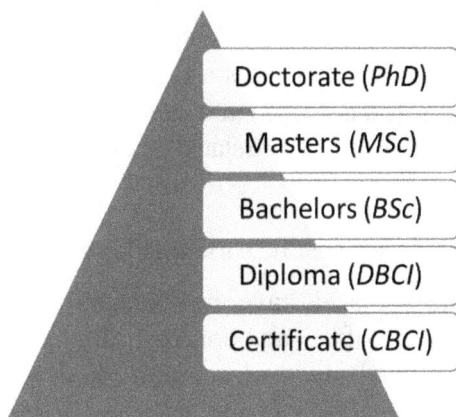

Figure 30: Example of academic business continuity qualifications

While this is not intended to be a definitive set of qualification options, it does provide an indication of what types of academic opportunities are available.

12.1 Certificate of the Business Continuity Institute

Taking a bottom up approach, we first have the Business Continuity Institute's Certificate (CBCI) which is a level four academic qualification. The BCI has partners around the world that deliver this five-day course which is based upon the good practice guidelines. The course is followed by a 120 multiple choice question exam paper. Please refer to *www.thebci.org/* for information about course providers.

12.2 Diploma of the Business Continuity Institute

The Business Continuity Institute's Diploma (DBCI) is a level five academic qualification and was developed by Buckinghamshire New University *http://bucks.ac.uk/* in conjunction with the BCI. This a distance learning course run over ten months and is broken into three modules. Students need to submit a 5,000 word BCM related report in the final module.

12.3 Bachelor's Degree in Business Continuity

I must confess that I have not noticed many academic institutions that offer an honours degree in Business Continuity, a level six qualification. However, one that I came across recently was the Rabdan Academy in Abu Dhabi: *http://rabdanacademy.ae* which offers a four year course, including work placement, that leads to a Bachelor of Science degree in BCM.

12.4 Master's Degree in Business Continuity

I studied for my level seven Master's degree at Buckinghamshire New University: *http://bucks.ac.uk*. At the time, it was called Business Continuity, Security and Emergency Management, although the title has recently been changed to Organisational Resilience. This is a two-year distance learning course

12.5 Doctorate in Business Continuity

For those students of business continuity who wish to progress to a doctorate level of academic achievement, there are a few universities that do offer the opportunity. Perhaps one worthy of mention is the University of Salford (*www.salford.ac.uk)*, which offers research opportunities in business continuity within its disaster management programme.

12.6 ISO22301 Certified Business Continuity Lead Auditor/Implementer

For those students looking to gain ISO22301 related qualifications, there are a number of organisations that offer training which leads to the Certified Business Continuity Management System Lead Auditor (*CBC LA*) or Lead Implementer (*CBC LI*). These courses and examinations would generally take five days or less.

CHAPTER 13: ADDITIONAL REFERENCE MATERIAL

13.1 Books

- **A Manager's Guide to ISO22301**, Tony Drewitt, 2013, Publisher: IT Governance Publishing, Cambridge
- **A Manager's Guide to ISO22301 Standard for Business Continuity Management System**, Goh Moh Heng, 2012, Publisher: GMH Pte Ltd, Singapore
- **Business Continuity for Dummies**, Sterling, S. et al., 2012, Publisher: John Wiley and Sons, Chichester
- **Business Continuity Institute's Good Practice Guidelines**, 2013, Publisher: The BCI, Caversham
- **In Hindsight – A compendium of Business Continuity Case Studies**, Robert Clark, 2014, Publisher: IT Governance Publishing, Cambridge
- **ISO22300** (and related publications), 2012, Publisher: BSI Standards, London
- **IT Disaster Recovery for Dummies**, Peter Gregory, 2008, Publisher: John Wiley and Sons
- **Testing and Exercising Your Business Continuity Plan**, Goh Moh Heng, 2006, Publisher: GMH Pte Ltd, Singapore
- **The Disaster Recovery Handbook,** Michael Wallace and Lawrence Webber, 2004, Amacom, New York
- **The Route Map to Business Continuity Management – Meeting the Requirements of ISO22301**, John Sharpe, 2012, Publisher: BSI, London

13.2 Videos

- **Practice Makes Perfect:** Exercising made easy – a comprehensive guide to exercising Business Continuity plans, the Business Continuity Institute, available from *www.thebci.org*

13.3 Games

- **BC24**, the Business Continuity Institute's online incident simulation game, available from *www.thebci.org*

CHAPTER 14: WORKS CITED

Abide, R., 2013. *Choosing an appropriate scenario for your business continuity plan exercises.* [Online]
Available at: *www.continuitycentral.com/feature1101.html*
[Accessed 15 12 2014].

Ap, T., 2014. *Five bank branches in Hong Kong shut due to Occupy Central disruptions.* [Online]
Available at: *www.scmp.com/business/banking-finance/article/1620489/five-bank-branches-hong-kong-shut-due-occupy-central*
[Accessed 28 12 2014].

Armit, T., 2007. BC Plan Testing. In: A. Hiles, ed. *The Definitive Handbook of Business Continuity Management.* 2nd ed. Chichester: Wiley, pp. 323-338.

Ashford, W., 2013. *Security experts welcome UK banking cyber attack test.* [Online]
Available at: *www.computerweekly.com/news/2240208779/Security-experts-welcome-UK-banking-cyber-attack-test*
[Accessed 13 06 2015].

Bank of England, 2013. *Waking Shark II - Exercise Scenario Injects.* [Online]
Available at: *www.bankofengland.co.uk/financialstability/fsc/Documents/ws2genericscenario.pdf*
[Accessed 14 06 2015].

BBC News, 2012. *Power shortage risks by 2015, Ofgem warns.* [Online]
Available at: *www.bbc.co.uk/news/business-19842401*
[Accessed 16 01 2015].

BBC News, 2014. *National Grid warns of lower winter power capacity.* [Online]
Available at: *www.bbc.co.uk/news/business-29794632*
[Accessed 16 01 2015].

BCI, 2010. *Good Practice Guidelines.* 2nd ed. Caversham: Business Continuity Institute.

BCI, 2013. *Good Practice Guidelines.* 3rd ed. Caversham: Business Continuity Institute.

BCI, 2015. *Guide to play the game.* [Online]
Available at: *www.bcifiles.com/BC24GuideFeb2014.pdf*
[Accessed 22 01 2015].

Beattie, J., 2014. *Preparing for disasters: 3 ways to improve your BC/DR Exercises.* [Online]
Available at: *www.forbes.com/sites/sungardas/2014/07/23/preparing-for-disaster-3-ways-to-improve-your-bcdr-exercises/*
[Accessed 25 11 2014].

Best, R., 1999. *Noah's Ark and the Ziusudra Epic: Sumerian Origins of the Flood Myth.* 1st ed. Fort Myers, FL: Enlil Press.

Brown, P., 2014. *University to test emergency lockdown system.* [Online]
Available at: *http://inside.uncc.edu/news/item/university-test-emergency-lockdown-system*
[Accessed 09 01 2015].

BSI, 2010. *PD 25666:2010 Business continuity.* 1st ed. s.l.:British Standards.

Byrd, L., 2015. *BCM Legislations, Regulations, Standards and Good Practice.* [Online]
Available at: *www.bcifiles.com/BCMLegislationsandRegulationsJan2014.pdf*
[Accessed 12 01 2015].

Chan, N., 2014. *Drill on Business Continuity Plans of the HKMA and banks.* [Online]
Available at: *www.hkma.gov.hk/eng/key-information/press-releases/2014/20140614-3.shtml*
[Accessed 28 12 2014].

Chetcuti, K., 2013. *Emergency Exercise at airport tests response.* [Online]
Available at: *www.timesofmalta.com/articles/view/20121113/local/Emergency-exercise-at-airport-tests-response.445147*
[Accessed 09 01 2015].

Clark, R., 2014. Aztec Chemicals Explosion, the biggest blaze in Cheshire for 35 years. In: R. Clark, ed. *In Hindsight - A compendium of Business Continuity case studies.* Cambridge, UK: IT Governance Publishing.

Clark, R. A., 2014. Northgate Information Services, a victim of the Buncefield oil depot disaster. In: R. A. Clark, ed. *In Hindsight - A compendium of Business Continuity case studies.* Cambridge, UK: IT Governance Publishing.

Continuity Central, 2006. *Business Continuity Quotations.* [Online]
Available at: *www.continuitycentral.com/feature0412.htm*
[Accessed 28 01 2015].

Dakin, C., 2014. The Gloucestershire Flooding 2007. In: R. Clark, ed. *In Hindsight - A compendium of Business Continuity case studies.* Cambridge, UK: IT Governance Publishing.

Dakin, C. & Jacobsen, J. S., 2014. Piper Alpha and Alexander L. Kielland: A Comparison of Two North Sea Tragedies. In: R. A. Clark, ed. *In Hindsight - A*

compendium of Business Continuity case studies.
Cambridge, UK: IT Governance Publishing.

Dartmouth College, 2012. *Dartmouth to Test Outdoor Mass Notification System on Thursday 23 February.* [Online]
Available at: *www.dartmouth.edu/~prepare/communications/omns-test.html*
[Accessed 28 01 2015].

Davison, M., 2014. *Waking Shark II: a curate's egg?.*
[Online]
Available at: *http://insights-on-business.com/banking/waking-shark-ii-a-curates-egg/*
[Accessed 14 06 2015].

Drewitt, T., 2013. *A Manager's Guide to ISO 22301.*
Cambridge, UK: IT Governance Publishing.

DSM Group, 2015. *Disaster Recovery Testing – Will Your Plan work?.* [Online]
Available at: *http://dsm-gb.co.uk/disaster-recovery-testing-will-your-plan-work/*
[Accessed 19 06 2015].

Eastbourne Herald, 2014. *Mock car bomb scare exercise in DGH grounds.* [Online]
Available at: *www.eastbourneherald.co.uk/news/local/mock-car-bomb-scare-exercise-in-dgh-grounds-1-6062799*
[Accessed 12 01 2015].

Edmonton International Airport, 2015. *Emergency Response Plan.* [Online]
Available at: *http://corporate.flyeia.com/about-us/emergency-response-services/emergency-response-plan*
[Accessed 01 02 2015].

Elliot, D., Swartz, E. & Harbane, B., 1999. *Business Continuity Management : Preparing for the worst.* 1st ed. United Kingdom: Incomes Data Services (acquired by Thomson Reuters in 2005).

FBI, 2013. *A Study of Active Shooter Incidents in the United States Between 2000 and 2013,* s.l.: FBI.

FBI, 2013b. *Active Shooter and Mass Casualty.* [Online] Available at: *www.fbi.gov/about-us/cirg/active-shooter-and-mass-casualty-incidents* [Accessed 13 03 2015].

FBI, 2014. *WMD Training - FBI Worst-Case Exercise Tests Response to Chemical Attack.* [Online] Available at: *www.fbi.gov/news/stories/2014/december/fbi-wmd-exercise-tests-response-to-chemical-attack/fbi-wmd-exercise-tests-response-to-chemical-attack* [Accessed 15 12 2014].

Feeney, C., 2014. The Devastating Effect of the SARS Pandemic on theTourism Industry. In: R. Clark, ed. *In Hindsight - a compendium of business continuity case studies.* Cambridge, UK: ITGP.

Finegan, S., 2013. *How Social Media can play havoc with your business continuity.* [Online] Available at: *www.manchester.gov.uk/downloads/download/5713/social_media_and_business_continuity* [Accessed 12 06 2015].

Fleming, S., 2013. *London prepares for the worst with cyber attack simulation.* [Online] Available at: *www.ft.com/cms/s/0/797fbd8e-4afe-11e3-8c4c-00144feabdc0.html#axzz3eBAqzb6i* [Accessed 01 06 2015].

Grady, J., 2014. *Cloud failures will happen. Are you ready?.* [Online]
Available at: *www.networkworld.com/article/2686975/public-cloud/cloud-failures-will-happen-are-you-ready.html*
[Accessed 19 06 2015].

Gregory, P., 2008. *IT Disaster Recovery for Dummies.* Hoboken, NJ: John Wiley and Sons.

Heart of London, 2015. *Training Events.* [Online]
Available at: *www.heartoflondonbid.london/business-resilience-2/business-preparation-events/*
[Accessed 12 06 2015].

Hicks, J., 2006. *PR Crisis Management - Tell It All, Tell It Fast And Tell The Truth.* [Online]
Available at: *http://ezinearticles.com/?PR-Crisis-Management---Tell-It-All,-Tell-It-Fast-And-Tell-The-Truth&id=204295*
[Accessed 22 05 2015].

Hook, R., 2013. *Ambulance crew take part in major Maltese airport accident training.* [Online]
Available at: *www.ambulancenews.com/ambulance_crew_take_part_in_major_maltese_airport_accident_training_13159.aspx*
[Accessed 09 01 2015].

ISO22301, 2012. *Societal Security - Business Continuity Management Systems - Requirements.* s.l.:BSI Stabdard Publications.

ISO22398, 2012. *Societal Security - Business Continuity Management Systems - Guidance.* London: BSI.

Jacque, R., 2010. *Plan Do Check Act (PDCA) – How it Applies To Business Continuity.* [Online]
Available at: *http://perspectives.avalution.com/2010/plan-do-check-act-pdca-%E2%80%93-how-it-applies-to-business-continuity-2/*
[Accessed 02 08 2015].

Keeling, C., 2013. *Waking Shark II Desktop Cyber Exercise – Report to participants.* [Online]
Available at: *www.bankofengland.co.uk/financialstability/fsc/Documents/wakingshark2report.pdf*
[Accessed 13 06 2015].

Kiras, j., 2014. *Suicide Bombing.* [Online]
Available at: *www.britannica.com/EBchecked/topic/736115/suicide-bombing*
[Accessed 30 12 2014].

Leydon, J., 2014. *We want it HARDER: City bankers survive simulated cyber-war.* [Online]
Available at: *www.theregister.co.uk/2014/02/06/waking_shark_ii_post_mortem/*
[Accessed 13 06 2015].

Mainmann, K., 2014. *Edmonton International Airport uses Twitter in mock bomb threat exercise.* [Online]
Available at: *www.edmontonsun.com/2014/05/27/edmonton-international-airport-holds-mock-bomb-threat-exercise*
[Accessed 12 01 2015].

Mistry, P., 2013. *Portsmouth Guildhall filledwith smoke for fire training exercise.* [Online]
Available at: *www.portsmouth.co.uk/news/local/portsmouth-guildhall-filled-with-smoke-for-exercise-1-4399797*
[Accessed 09 01 2015].

Murray, A., 2013. *Andy Murray Heart breaks down at Dunblane memory !!! Wimbledon 2013* [Interview] 2013.

Nadel, B., 2012. *We review five of the best-known cloud-based backup services.* [Online]
Available at: *www.computerworld.com/article/2500640/data-center/5-online-backup-services-keep-your-data-safe.html*
[Accessed 11 06 2015].

Pearson, G. & Woodman, P., 2012. *Planning for the worst.* [Online]
Available at: *http://shop.bsigroup.com/upload/BCM%20Report%202012.pdf*
[Accessed 03 03 2014].

Project Griffin, 2014. *Protecting our communities.* [Online]
Available at: *www.projectgriffin.org.uk/*
[Accessed 24 06 2015].

Regester, M. & Larkin, J., 2008. *Risk Issues and Crisis Management in Public Relations.* Fourth ed. London and Philadelphia: CIPR.

Royal Institution of Naval Architects, 2014. *Fire at Sea.* [Online]
Available at: *www.rina.org.uk/fire-at-sea.html*
[Accessed 18 01 2015].

Royal Navy, 2015. *Firefighting Training.* [Online]
Available at: *www.royalnavy.mod.uk/our-organisation/where-we-are/training-establishments/hms-excellent/firefighting-training*
[Accessed 17 01 2015].

Shakespeare, W., 1597. *Romeo and Julliet.* Stratford-upon-Avon: s.n.

Sterling, S. et al., 2012. *Business Continuity for Dummies.* Chichester: John Wiley and Sons.

Tehrani, N., 2004. *Workplace trauma: concepts, assessment, and interventions..* Brighton: Brunner-Routledge.

The Business Continuity Consultant, 2015. *Failure to exercise.* [Online]
Available at: *https://merrycon.wordpress.com/category/ business-continuity/*
[Accessed 02 08 2015].

The WHO, 2013. *Pandemic Influenza Risk Management : WHO Interim Guidance.* [Online]
Available at: *www.who.int/influenza/preparedness/ pandemic/GIP_PandemicInfluenzaRiskManagementInterim Guidance_Jun2013.pdf*
[Accessed 02 04 2015].

Varley, B., 2010. *Creating Effective Business Cntinuity Plans.* [Online]
Available at: *www.continuitycentral.com/feature0258.htm*
[Accessed 12 12 2014].

Wayne State University, 2015. *Today@Wayne.* [Online]
Available at: *http://today.wayne.edu/featured-stories/17496*
[Accessed 02 04 2015].

Wood, P., 2012. *Resilient Thinking - Protecting organisations in the 21st century.* 1st ed. Cambridge: IT Governance Publishing.

CHAPTER 15: GLOSSARY

ITEM	EXPLANATION
(E)DM system	Electronic Data Management system
9/11	9/11 is the shorthand name given to the terrorist attacks that occurred in the US on 11 September 2001 in which almost 3,000 people lost their lives
9-Track	The 9-Track tape and tape drive is a magnetic tape and was released by IBM in the 1960s as part of the IBM system 360 mainframe computer range
A&C	Appraisal and Counselling
A/S 400	A mid-range IBM computer first released in the late 1980s
Apps	An App is a computer program designed to run on smartphones and tablet computers
APT	Advanced Persistent Threat – a computer network penetration in which an unauthorised person gains access to a network, remaining there undetected for prolonged periods, usually with the primary objective of stealing data rather than causing damage
Argus	Also known as Project Argus is a UK Government counter terrorism initiative that provides counter terrorism and security awareness training for business
ATM	Automatic Teller Machine
Battle Box	Contains anything deemed necessary dealing with an incident, such as a BCP (plus other related plans), keys, software licence info, contact lists of staff and suppliers, etc.

BC24	A business continuity simulation game created by the BCI
BCI	Business Continuity Institute
BCM	Business Continuity Management
BCMS	Business Continuity Management System
BCP	Business Continuity Plan
BIA	Business Impact Analysis
BoE	Bank of England
BS	British Standard
Call tree	Sometimes referred to as a telephone tree. It is a list of people to be notified of an event/incident occurring
CATSA	Canadian Air Transport Security Authority
CBC LA / LI	Certified Business Continuity Lead Auditor/Lead Implementer
CBCI	Certificate of the Business Continuity Institute, a level '4' qualification
CBRN	Chemical, Biological, Radiological and Nuclear. So far there have been terrorist attacks that have used 'CBR' but as yet no use of nuclear weapons
CEO	Chief Executive Officer
CISP Platform	Cyber-Security Information Sharing Partnership
CPD	Civil Protection Department – the Maltese fire and rescue service
DBCI	Diploma of the Business Continuity Institute, a level '5' qualification
DEA	Drug Enforcement Administration
DR	Disaster Recovery
EIA	Edmonton International Airport

FBCS	Fellow of the British Computer Society
FBI	Federal Bureau of Investigation
FIBCM	Fellow of the Institute of Business Continuity Management
FRS	Fire and Rescue Service (UK)
FTP	File Transfer Protocol – a standard network protocol for transferring files from one host computer to another host computer using a TCP-based network
Gigabyte	A byte is a unit of digital information that equates to one alphanumeric character. A Gigabyte is one billion (10^9) bytes
GPG	Good Practice Guidelines
HKMA	Hong Kong Monetary Authority
ICT (IT)	Information and Communication Technology sometimes referred to as IT – Information Technology
IRA	Irish Republican Army
ISO	International Standards Organisation
IT (ICT)	Information Technology sometimes referred to as ICT – Information and Communication Technology
ITIL	Information Technology Infrastructure Library
ITSM	Information Technology Service Management
KPI's	Key Performance Indicators
LPG	Liquid Petroleum Gas
MBCI	Member of the Business Continuity Institute
MCA	Marine and Coastguard Agency (UK)
MDH	Mater Dei Hospital, Republic of Malta

Megabyte	A byte is a unit of digital information that equates to one alphanumeric character. A Megabyte is one million (10^6) bytes
MWE	Market Wide Exercise
MSyI	Member of the Security Institute
MTPD	Maximum Tolerable Period of Disruption
NaCTSO	National Counter Terrorism Security Advisor (UK)
Occupy Central	This is a Hong Kong based civil disobedience movement whose objective is to pressure the Government of the Peoples' Republic of China into granting universal suffrage
OFGEM	Regulates the electricity and gas markets in Great Britain
OMNS	Outdoor Mass Notification System that typically uses sirens and an audio public address system to warn people of an emergency
PA	Public Address (Loud speaker system)
PAS	Publically Available Standard
PC	Personal Computer
PPS	Police and Public Safety Department
Q&A	Question and Answer
QA	Quality Assurance
QM	Quality Management
RCMP	Royal Canadian Mounted Police
RTO	Recovery Time Objective
SME	Small and Medium size Enterprise

15: Glossary

SMS	Short Message Service also referred to as a Text Message is a component of a mobile phone messaging system
Terabyte	A byte is a unit of digital information that equates to one alphanumeric character. A Terabyte is one trillion (10^{12}) bytes
The Cloud	Despite what some individuals seem to believe, Cloud computing is not magical or mystical. Simplistically it means storing and accessing data via the Internet rather than using your own in-house hardware
UNC	University of North Carolina
WMD	Weapons of Mass Destruction which is a term often used to refer to Chemical, Biological, Radiological and Nuclear (CBRN) weapons
HVAC	Heating, Ventilation and Air Conditioning system

CHAPTER 16: FREE TEMPLATE DOWNLOADS

A number of validation related templates are available to download free of charge at:

www.bcm-consultancy.com/templates

ITG RESOURCES

IT Governance Ltd sources, creates and delivers products and services to meet the real-world, evolving IT governance needs of today's organisations, directors, managers and practitioners.

The ITG website (*www.itgovernance.co.uk*) is the international one-stop-shop for corporate and IT governance information, advice, guidance, books, tools, training and consultancy. On the website you will find the following page related to the subject matter of this book:

www.itgovernance.co.uk/bc_dr.aspx.

Publishing Services

IT Governance Publishing (ITGP) is the world's leading IT-GRC publishing imprint that is wholly owned by IT Governance Ltd.

With books and tools covering all IT governance, risk and compliance frameworks, we are the publisher of choice for authors and distributors alike, producing unique and practical publications of the highest quality, in the latest formats available, which readers will find invaluable.

www.itgovernancepublishing.co.uk is the website dedicated to ITGP. Other titles published by ITGP that may be of interest include:

- Disaster Recovery and Business Continuity

  www.itgovernance.co.uk/shop/p-520-disaster-recovery-and-business-continuity-third-edition.aspx

- A Manager's Guide to ISO22301

  www.itgovernance.co.uk/shop/p-331-a-managers-guide-to-iso22301.aspx

- Business Continuity Management: Choosing to Survive

  www.itgovernance.co.uk/shop/p-412-business-continuity-management-choosing-to-survive.aspx.

- In Hindsight: A compendium of Business Continuity case studies

  www.itgovernance.co.uk/shop/p-1621-in-hindsight-a-compendium-of-business-continuity-case-studies.aspx

We also offer a range of off-the-shelf toolkits that give comprehensive, customisable documents to help users create the specific documentation they need to properly implement a management system or standard. Written by experienced practitioners and based on the latest best practice, ITGP toolkits can save months of work for organisations working towards compliance with a given standard.

For further information please review the following pages:

- ISO22301 BCMS Implementation Toolkit

  www.itgovernance.co.uk/shop/p-1039.aspx

- Full range of toolkits

  www.itgovernance.co.uk/shop/c-129-toolkits.aspx.

Books and tools published by IT Governance Publishing (ITGP) are available from all business booksellers and the following websites:

www.itgovernance.eu   *www.itgovernanceusa.com*

www.itgovernance.in   *www.itgovernancesa.co.za*

www.itgovernance.asia.

Training Services

A business continuity plan necessarily involves the whole organisation so staff training is essential to its success. Our range of ISO 22301 courses offers a structured learning path from Foundation to Advanced level, with qualifications awarded by IBITGQ.

The ISO 22301 Learning Pathway includes:

- **ISO22301 Certified BCMS Foundation**

  www.itgovernance.co.uk/shop/p-694-iso22301-certified-bcms-foundation-training-course.aspx.

- **ISO22301 Certified BCMS Lead Implementer**

  www.itgovernance.co.uk/shop/p-695-iso22301-certified-bcms-lead-implementer-training-course.aspx.

- **ISO22301 Certified BCMS Lead Auditor**

IT Governance's practical, hands-on approach to ISO 22301 training is delivered by experienced practitioners who focus on improving your knowledge, developing your skills, and awarding relevant, industry-recognised certifications. Our fully integrated and structured Learning Pathway accommodates delegates with various levels of knowledge, and our courses can be delivered in a variety of formats to suit all delegates.

For more information about IT Governance's ISO 222301 training courses, please see: *www.itgovernance.co.uk/iso22301-courses.aspx.*

For information on any of our many other courses, including ISO 27001 and information security, PCI DSS compliance, IT governance, service management, and professional certification courses, please see: *www.itgovernance.co.uk/training.aspx.*

Professional Services and Consultancy

ISO 22301 is the international standard for business continuity management. Deploying an ISO 22301-compliant business continuity management system (BCMS) will allow your organisation to demonstrate to its customers, suppliers, shareholders and staff that it has taken a best-practice approach to preparing for disruptive incidents.

Implementing ISO 22301 is, however, a complex undertaking. Our business continuity experts can save you hours of uncertainty, and trial and error, by providing your organisation with the core competence and skills it needs in order to implement a BCMS and/or achieve ISO 22301 certification in the shortest timeframe possible.

We offer fixed-price and bespoke consultancy options, depending on your organisation's needs and requirements, including:

- **Business Continuity Management/ISO 22301 Health Check**

  www.itgovernance.co.uk/shop/p-1630-business-continuity-management-iso-22301-health-check.aspx.

- **FastTrack™ Business Continuity Management/ISO 22301**

  www.itgovernance.co.uk/shop/p-1631-fasttrack-business-continuity-management-iso-22301-consultancy.aspx.

For more information on our ISO 22301 consultancy service, please see: *www.itgovernance.co.uk/iso22301-consultancy.aspx.*

For general information about our other consultancy services, including for ISO 20000, ISO 27001, Cyber Essentials, the PCI DSS, Data Protection and more, please see: *www.itgovernance.co.uk/consulting.asp.*

Newsletter

IT governance is one of the hottest topics in business today, not least because it is also the fastest moving.

You can stay up to date with the latest developments across the whole spectrum of IT governance subject matter, including; risk management, information security, ITIL and IT service management, project governance, compliance and so much more, by subscribing to ITG's core publications and topic alert emails.

Simply visit our subscription centre and select your preferences: *www.itgovernance.co.uk/newsletter.aspx*.

EU for product safety is Stephen Evans, The Mill Enterprise Hub, Stagreenan, Drogheda, Co. Louth, A92 CD3D, Ireland. (servicecentre@itgovernance.eu)